# SHEPHERD OF THE BLACK SHEEP

MEMOIRS OF AN ALASKAN MISSIONARY

By Alan L. Pearce

Mr. Pearce loves to hear from his readers.  If you have enjoyed this book, or if God has spoken to you or encouraged you through it, or if you have any questions about the book or about the Christian life it describes, please feel free to contact him directly:

Pearce@ShepherdoftheBlackSheep.com

or via his website:

www.ShepherdoftheBlackSheep.com.

© Copyright 2012-13 by Alan L. Pearce
Anderson, South Carolina
All rights reserved.

ISBN-13:
978-1490398174

## IN HONOR AND REMEMBRANCE OF

# TROY TURNER

It's March 29th, 2003 and I just got home after a hard day at work. It's time to go to services for my buddy Troy Turner. Troy was from Indiana right near a place where my grandmother, who was a Turner, had some people. I always claimed Troy as a cousin. He was fighting for his life from the time I met him. He had hepatitis and never got a liver transplant.

Troy was a rock of Gibraltar. He leaves an awfully big hole now that he's gone. He never complained, he never questioned why. He never rebuked God or doctors or anyone else. He had a beautiful spirit. He didn't say a lot, but when he said something you had to listen because when Troy spoke he had something worth listening to.

Troy was a part of our home group, at Butch's, out at Midway Community Church. He was a carpenter and Butch made that comparison when Troy came to follow Jesus, who was a carpenter. Troy went on with his life, was always positive, always looked for the good in people.

I miss Troy, but I know he's with his Lord. He never ever wavered in that faith; never questioned. He knew where he was going. He loved and cared for his family. He loved his church. He loved everyone in the church. He was a special blessing to all of us because when he was so sick he'd still come to church if he could and he still encouraged us.

I think he handled his sickness a lot better than we did. Many times we cried and prayed for Troy. He was a man among men, probably the greatest encourager that I've met in my life. And every time I'd try to encourage him, he'd pour it back on me and encourage me so much more. It stretched and strengthened my faith because of his abundant trust and ability to relax and let God have control.

At the services today Mike Noland sang "If You Could See Me Now", and we tried to visualize when Troy and Jesus met face to face. God is so good. Trust Him in all circumstances. Usually when things look pretty bad, you can look around and see somebody who has it worse. I don't know that Troy really could, and he never did. He always said God had been good to him and he blessed those that he could with his life, his testimony, his smile, his encouragement, his love for the Lord and his love for the church.

Miss you Troy, God bless. I know you're with Him.

(Editor's note: Troy's encouragement was a major factor in the completion of this book.)

## FOREWORD

When Al and his wife were out on deputation for their mission work in Alaska, I received a call from the pastor of a church where they were speaking. The pastor and his church were of a mind to support their effort. My name had been provided as a reference.

The pastor asked me several questions about Al and his qualifications, but it all came down to whether a guy with a police background could make the switch to a missionary life style. I told him it wouldn't make any difference. The pastor was taken aback by this statement, but came around as I explained it.

There wouldn't be any change because Al already was a missionary. If you talked to me for 30 minutes it is likely that we would be talking about flying. Al and I had a lot of competition with each other over our flying. Who had what rating. Who had the most hours. But if you talked to Al for 30 minutes you would be talking about the Lord. If Al saw you with a broken down car he'd get under there to help you fix it. But before you were finished you would have been brought face to face with the good news of God's Grace.

What you see in Al is what you get. That is what you will find in South Carolina. That is what you find in Alaska. That is what you will find in this book. No pretense, nothing feigned...just a man with a deep love for Jesus and a burden for those who do not know Him.

# CONTENTS

**CHAPTER** | | **PAGE**

| | Dedication | 3 |
| | Foreword | 5 |
| 1 | Baseletez | 8 |
| 2 | First Day in Alaska | 9 |
| 3 | Lion Hunt in Alaska | 11 |
| 4 | Another Dumb White Man | 13 |
| 5 | Black Jeans | 20 |
| 6 | Where Would Jesus Be? | 23 |
| 7 | Time | 26 |
| 8 | A Day in the Life of a Bush Missionary | 28 |
| 9 | Moose Hunting in Alaska | 31 |
| 10 | James 5:14 | 36 |
| 11 | What are you worth? | 39 |
| 12 | CESSNA 170 | 41 |
| 13 | Alaska Air Mail | 44 |
| 14 | Nothing Wasted | 48 |
| 15 | Homestead Property Line | 52 |
| 16 | A Divine Interruption | 54 |
| 17 | Cheechaco | 64 |
| 18 | The Snake Hunt | 67 |
| 19 | Don | 69 |
| 20 | A Bad Example | 72 |
| 21 | Potlatch | 75 |
| 22 | Lee | 78 |
| 23 | The Mechanic | 80 |
| 24 | Time to Look Up | 82 |
| 25 | The Fighter | 87 |

## CONTENTS CONTINUED

| CHAPTER | | PAGE |
|---|---|---|
| 26 | The Missionary and the Mouse | 89 |
| 27 | Big John | 92 |
| 28 | Ole | 100 |
| 29 | Perspective | 105 |
| 30 | Chistochina Gold | 107 |
| 31 | Bear? | 111 |
| 32 | Hitchhiker | 114 |
| 33 | Mr. Belt | 119 |
| 34 | The Most Anti-Social Man I Ever Met | 125 |
| 35 | Eglick | 128 |
| 36 | Shanan | 129 |
| 37 | Last Flight in Alaska | 130 |
| 38 | Leaving Out | 133 |
| 39 | I Am My Brother's Keeper | 157 |
| 40 | Be Sure Your Sins Will Find You Out | 160 |
| 41 | Wounded Soldier | 166 |
| 42 | Great is Thy Faithfulness | 175 |

| | |
|---|---|
| *PHOTOS* | 193 |
| *EPILOGUE: RETURN TO ALASKA* | 196 |
| *ACKNOWLEDGEMENTS* | 204 |

## CHAPTER ONE

## BASELETEZ

My journey started in Streator, Illinois May 17th, 1945. And at the time of this writing it has included wanderings to Massachusetts and Pennsylvania, Rhode Island and South Carolina, back up to Illinois for a little while and back to South Carolina, Alabama thrown in there, and a trip to Alaska for three years. Many of the stories come out of Alaska.

The name of this chapter comes from the Indian name that the Athabascan Indians gave me there. Baseletez, means Dall sheep. They said I went to the high places and the hard places. God blessed me with the opportunity to serve in an area covered by 112 miles of highways and homes and cabins off the road. I got to every home at least once. I got thrown out of some and got welcomed at some, got ignored at others, but God was good for they were to see God's work in a little chapel in Chistochina and Slana and I am still blessed with wonderful Christian friends from that area who keep in touch.

## CHAPTER TWO

## FIRST DAY IN ALASKA

When I was about 12 years old I told my momma after watching the Jim Elliott life story, <u>Through Gates of Splendor</u>, that I wanted to be a missionary pilot in Alaska. I didn't get my first flying lesson until I was 34 years old, but by the time I was 41 I was on the road to Alaska as a missionary pilot with Send International of Alaska.

The night we got to Glennallen, after driving about eight days in a 26-foot U-Haul truck, pulling our old '78 Mercury Cougar, we unloaded the truck at the apartment we would stay in during our training and orientation.

I took the truck down the road to the U-Haul dealer, the only one in town, and dropped it off. Everybody else was tired and went to bed but I was just happy to be the last guy walking around, kicking dirt and just looking. It was Alaska.

I love Alaska and I love people. I just started walking. Glennallen is about 10 miles long and 300 feet wide and there's a business on each side of the road with a few vacant lots here and there, a couple of little side streets, nothing of any account. But I started out and walked down the road, stopping at each business, talking to people and having a good time.

When I got to the end, I crossed the street and started back. I noticed there were some new people up the road at some places I had been to, so I zigzagged back and forth across the street having a high old time.

By the time I got back to the apartment everybody was looking for me. I had been gone 37 hours. I hadn't thought at all about the fact that the sun doesn't set in Alaska in June. I had a blast and met a lot of wonderful people and I just got lost. Of course, when I went to bed that first day/night, or whatever it was in Alaska, I slept a long time, but I had had a lot of fun.

## CHAPTER THREE

## LION HUNT IN ALASKA

I met a guy who, at the time that Alaska became a state, became an Alaska State Trooper. Also when Alaska became a state, Sears Roebuck built the first shopping mall in Anchorage. It consisted of a Sears store and just a couple of other stores.

To celebrate statehood and the grand opening, Sears brought a circus to town complete with a lion tamer show. They set up a couple of days before the show would start.

The guy who was in charge of feeding the lions loved to fish, and somebody took him salmon fishing. Salmon were running and he was catching big salmon, having a blast. He was gone two days because he didn't realize that the sun doesn't set in Alaska in June.

So the poor lion didn't get anything to eat and he broke out of his cage. The first thing he came to that smelled good was a little girl with a corndog. The lion ate the corndog and mauled the girl.

The State Trooper I had met was carrying a Smith &Wesson .38 special, four-inch barrel. He shot that lion six times. Every time he'd shoot it, the lion would fall down dead and then roll over and come right back up the way he did in the show. He wasn't hurting that lion much at all.

So he grabbed another Trooper's revolver when that Trooper froze and didn't shoot and he shot him six more times. The lion would go down, roll over and come back up.

So he ran to his car and grabbed an M-2 Carbine, which is a fully automatic .30 caliber with a 50-round magazine. He came back and ripped off 50 rounds and killed the lion. The bullets ricocheted off the pavement and took all of the windows out of the new shopping center.

He got commended by the Governor of the state of Alaska for saving the little girl's life. He got sued by Sears for busting all their windows, and he got three-days suspension for not being able to account for all his ammunition.

He said, "You've got to be good to get suspended for the same thing that the governor gives you commendation for."

The happy ending to the story was the little girl became a good friend of his and he became good friends with her family. And when her father passed away before she married she asked the State Trooper to give her away at the wedding. When they had the wedding, the Anchorage newspaper did a full-page spread on the whole thing, showing the dead lion and the man and the commendation and the lawsuit and the suspension and showing the little girl as she went through her surgeries.

So the story did have a happy ending, and it's just one of those funny things that could only happen in Alaska.

## CHAPTER FOUR

## JUST ANOTHER DUMB WHITE MAN

They sent me to Chistochina to work in a village. Time and again they'd had a resident pastor living in Chistochina. Other times people commuted and the work was not going extremely well when I got there.

One of my first friends among the natives was Jack John Justin. He was a great big fellow, probably about 6'3", 240 pounds, gray hair and blue eyes. When you say a native has blue eyes that tells you that he's got some white blood in him. Actually his mother was a white woman. The natives might call somebody half breed if they're mad at them, but if they respect them and they have white blood they'll just say they have blue eyes. I've heard them tell this. Some men had blue eyes and I'd look at them and their eyes were brown as could be. So they're not talking about the color of his eyes, they're talking about the blood content. They're talking about him having mixed blood.

Jack lived in a cabin right off the runway at Chistochina. Chistochina means first waters. It's the headwater of the Copper River where the Chistochina and Slana Rivers meet and flow in the Copper River. It's a beautiful location.

The main street of town, at least during hunting and fishing season, was the runway. Everybody came and went by plane when they were going out to hunt or to fish. There were a lot of

Super Cubs with Cessna 206's, and 185's and 180's quite often.

Jack sort of took me to his heart. He'd come and talk with me. And one Sunday I got up to preach and only the white folks showed up. There wasn't a single native in the place. Well, I'm real sharp. I figured out that there was a problem here and I'd done something that offended the natives.

So as soon as the service was over, I went home and ate dinner and trudged across the road to talk to Jack. I went in and said, "Jack, I feel I've offended your people in some way. I didn't mean to do it. Help me understand your people. Teach me about your people. God loves them and I love them and I don't want to hurt them. I want to learn to do right, to bring them to Jesus and bring Jesus to them."

Jack told me to sit down. I sat down at the table and he sat at the table and we just sat. We sat for a few minutes and he said, "Suppose you have to borrow something from your neighbor and the white man runs in and says I need a cup of sugar; give me a cup of sugar. That tells the native that your party is more important than them."

He said, "If you have to borrow a cup of sugar, you go sit down with the neighbor and you talk a while and let them talk about what they want to talk about, tell you what's happening in their lives and what they're thinking and whatever they have to say. And then when you're ready to go, just almost like an afterthought, you say could I borrow a cup of sugar. You've shown them that they're important in your eyes and they'll be glad to help you." That was a valuable lesson and it taught me a lot.

And then we just sat. We sat there for probably close to an hour. He didn't say a thing. Somebody knocked on the door and he just looked at the door and didn't say come in or anything else. Directly the person knocked again. He got up and walked over to the door and said, "Another dumb white man." It was one of the local mechanics who needed something.

What Jack was telling me was in Alaska when you come to a native home and you knock on the door the knock on the door is just to announce that you're coming in. Just go in; don't make the people drop everything they're doing to come open the door for you. If they don't want you in, they'll lock the door. If the door is open go on in. And I found out that on a lot of occasions I was just one of those dumb white men.

Jack John Justin is a precious brother in the Lord. He was saved on a mountainside when he experienced a bad winter and heavy snows. The caribou and the sheep herds hadn't moved. He had a family to feed and couldn't find anything. Jack was a hunter, he was a good hunter. Even up to 82, 83 years old he was shooting caribou with a .30/.30 with iron sights and he'd shoot him at 100 yards and bring home the meat.

Jack told me the story how he got up on the mountain and the snow was pretty heavy and it was late in the season. Well, actually it was early snow, but it was late in the hunting season. Sheep hadn't moved that year. He sat down on a rock and he said, "God, I don't know who You are and how to talk to You, but my family is hungry, I need sheep." He said just a couple minutes later he looked up and there was a sheep and he shot it.  As he approached to skin it out, he realized there were no tracks in the snow.  He believed it was a miracle from God; that God just dropped a sheep for him for his family.

He went back and fed the family and then hitched up a dog team and went on into Glennallen and talked with a missionary and told him what had happened and asked him how he could have a relationship with God.  The rest of his life Jack John Justin walked with Jesus as his Lord and Savior.  He taught me a lot about that too.  I was just another dumb white man that he helped.  Thank God for Jack's life.

Several years after I left Alaska I got the message that he had passed away and I spoke with some of the people in the village.  They implanted a pacemaker in Jack's heart and he had to go back into town.  He was 84, I believe, and his eyes were failing and he was having more problems.  So he went to the native hospital.  They told him they were going to have to change the battery in his pacemaker.  He said, "No, I want to go home."  They said, "Well you can't go home.  If you go home, something's going to happen and you're just going to die."  But he said, "I want to go home.

He was talking about wanting to go home to be with Jesus.  He wasn't suicidal, but he'd just gone through all the surgeries and medical procedures that he cared to go through in his life.  He was content.  He was ready to walk with Jesus.

He went home and not too many days later he went to sleep and woke up in Jesus' arms.  I still miss him.  I was just another dumb white man that he helped. Thank God for Jack's life. Jack was a very special friend.

The native people say that they heard the raven call their name. That was an old native legend. That was their way of saying that it's your time to go. Jack heard Jesus call his name.

Anyway, back to the Sunday afternoon in the cabin.... When the old fellow got what he needed and left and didn't show him the courtesy of waiting on him and talking to him, he just came in like a white man and grabbed what he needed and ran. Jack just looked and sat.

It was probably another hour we sat there and Jack looked at the clock and he said, "I've got to go feed my dog. You come back tomorrow and I'll teach you more." I was a little flabbergasted. He taught me one thing and showed me one thing and for two hours I sat and he never said a word.

I went home and called old Jim Johnson, who was one of the older missionaries in Glennallen. He worked with the native people. In fact, he was one of the few who knew a little of the Athabascan language. He knew and loved the people. I called him and said, "Jim, I need help." He said, "What's going on?" I said, "No natives came to church this morning. I went over to see Jack John Justin and asked him to help teach me so I wouldn't do wrong again and run off the natives we're trying to reach. We sat for two hours and never said anything and told me to come back tomorrow and he'd teach me more." Jim was elated. He said, "Wow, that's great."

I thought I had gone to a senile native who forgot he was supposed to teach me something and didn't teach me anything and now I'm talking to a senile missionary. They think I should learn something and nobody said a word. And finally Jim said, "Al, the native people are quiet. When you want to learn about the native people, sit. They'll tell you what they want you to know in time. You show them the respect of sitting and waiting on them and they'll show you all the respect they can."

In fact, at the home when someone has passed away, you come and you sit and you sit quietly. And you hug them when you come in and you give them a very gentle handshake because the natives don't squeeze hands, they just touch hands. But you just sit and wait and you let them talk and let them spill their grief. Sometimes you'll sit for several days before the person wants to really talk. When they want to talk, you listen.

So Jack was teaching me valuable lessons and I was just another dumb white man that thought you had to have a lesson plan and talk and point things out and illustrate things to teach. He was teaching in the native way, at which he was so adept. He taught a lot of the younger natives the old ways. He taught many of the white people who wanted to learn, who loved the natives.

I think Jack was probably the one who gave me the name Baseletez, Dall sheep. He said I went to the high places, the hard places where others didn't go because I went to every cabin and home in my area telling them about Jesus.

When my dad came to town to visit (it was the only trip he made to Alaska and I was so thankful that he came) he and Jack became the best of friends. They just shared their Christian lives. They shared their personal lives. They were kindred spirits. I was so glad for that. That's another native way. If you really love a person, you also honor their family, their parents, and their kids. The natives are very much into a friend of a friend is a friend, or the family of a friend is a friend. That's important in their way of life. It's important in the Christian way of life. There's no room for prejudice in the native culture and there's no room for it in the Christian life.

## CHAPTER FIVE

# BLACK JEANS

The mission didn't know what to do with me when I got there. There were several things that had changed and they needed me as a church planter rather than as a pilot. So the flying I did in Alaska was sort of secondary to working with the men and especially out in the villages. I flew a little bit for the mission, but mostly I was out in the bush as a church planter.

I was probably their problem child when I first arrived. I guess I didn't fit the molds real good and time and again they would call me to go into Glennallen and I would drive 50 miles to have them explain to me how I had to do things differently.

It comes to mind that one time they called me in and they said to me that I was being a bad example to the natives. That concerned me because I didn't want to be a bad example to anybody. I asked them what they thought I was doing wrong. They said, "Well, we understand that you're preaching in blue jeans." Well, they were right, I was preaching in blue jeans. For most of the men in the village blue jeans were all that they had to wear. In that culture a man kept a bolo tie, a little string tie with some kind of a clasp or a medallion on it, and he'd put that over his flannel shirt and he was dressed up. In blue jeans and a flannel shirt and a bolo tie, he'd go to weddings or funerals or anything else that happened to come about. So I pretty much dressed the way they did.

Well, I tried to persuade them that I was trying to deal with spiritual conditions and not set a fashion trend. But they said, "Well, don't preach in blue jeans anymore." So, being very obedient to those in authority over me, I pulled out of the driveway and instead of turning left and going to Chistochina I hung a right and went on down the road to Anchorage, which was about 140 or 150 miles away. There I went to Sam's Club and bought me a pair of black jeans.

So Sunday morning everybody had already heard, as mission gossip got around the valley pretty quickly, that I was not to preach in blue jeans. They wanted to see what was going to happen so when I stepped in church Sunday morning there were quite a few extras. I don't remember the attendance figure, as I never kept those numbers. It's like Butch says, "Nickels and noses aren't the things you need anyway."

But as I stepped in that morning in my fresh crisp black jeans, the people in the chapel waiting stood up and clapped. I guess they knew my heart was with them and I didn't want to embarrass them in any way, but I also had to obey the people who sign my paycheck and the people who were my elders in that situation. So whenever I preached, conducted a Bible study, or had a wedding or a funeral I would wear black jeans. There were a few occasions where I did wear a coat and tie because the family of those getting married or being buried felt better in that, but other than that my preaching attire was a flannel shirt and black jeans.

The lesson here is that there are a lot of churches and a lot of places where you have to dress right and you have to follow the current fashions and you have to fit in with a certain standard. God doesn't look at our clothing. There's many a man in tattered rags who is clothed in righteousness before Almighty God because he's turned to God in grace and asked Jesus Christ to forgive him of his sins and come into his life. I'm not saying clothes are not important, but they are not what is important to God. Come as you are, Jesus loves you.

## CHAPTER SIX

## WHERE WOULD JESUS BE?

I really didn't go to Alaska to the mission field to frustrate those who were in charge, but I think I may have done that. God made me a unique person, weird or strange or whatever you want to call it, but that's okay. God's put me through a whole bunch of unusual situations. It made me the person I am today and I thank Him that I came to know Jesus at an early age and that I grew up in a Christian home. My father was a pastor and I learned so much of living God's way.

Daddy didn't teach legalism. He believed that we were saved by grace through faith; that is not of ourselves, but as a gift of God, not of works. That theology gives you a lot more freedom to work in unorthodox ways. I didn't have to worry about losing points for going to the wrong place or looking like the wrong thing. I just prayed and walked with God to the best of my ability and Jesus lived through me.

The mission called me again down to Glennallen from Chistochina. I had to go down there and the person in charge spoke with me about where I spent Saturday nights. And where I spent Saturday nights was in the Chistochina Lodge.

In Alaska every village has a lodge, and that lodge is a gas station and grocery store, a motel, sometimes a restaurant and most always a bar. Chistochina had a really unique lodge. It was an old lodge and since has burned to the ground and been rebuilt.

In the back of the bar they had a pool table. I've always enjoyed playing pool. One of the burdens of my heart for the Alaskan church was to see men involved in it. I firmly believe that if men are going to be involved in the church, the preacher has to be a man in the community. If he goes and has tea and visits with the ladies while the men are out working and leaves them a message that he'd like to see them in church, there's a very good chance he never will.

But by Saturday nights after the sermon was prepared and everything was pretty much in line for the next day-- and of course in the winter time after I had started the fire to supplement the oil heat, I'd walk across the road and get a Dr. Pepper. I like Dr. Pepper, but I also know that there's no alcoholic beverage that comes in a purple can and no one would ever see me drinking a Dr. Pepper and mistakenly believe it was an alcoholic beverage and maybe cause somebody to stumble. I'd get a Dr. Pepper and I'd go play pool back there in the back of the bar. And time and again somebody would say, "Well preacher what you going to preach on tomorrow?" And I'd say, "Well, service time is 11 o'clock. If you want to know what I'm going to preach on, come on over. You're invited. I'd love to have you". A number of the men from the lodge did come over there and we saw some get saved and some get active in the church. I saw a bunch of Jonah's, a bunch of people running away from God. They got their hearts in line with God's program and they began to live for Him and that was great encouragement.

Anyway, back to the story. The mission said we understand that you are in the bar at the Chistochina Lodge on Saturday nights and wondered why you would do that. I thought, just a minute now. I told him, "I'm there because if Jesus Christ was physically present in Chistochina on Saturday night that's where He'd be because He loves men as well as women and He loves all men and wants to reach all men for Himself to be a part of the church, the body of Christ, not just securing a heavenly home for eternity, but giving people a purpose in life and reaching others and serving Him."

They didn't say anymore. They didn't tell me I couldn't go, so I continued the rest of my time in Chistochina. I spent Saturday nights back there in the back of the bar playing pool. And sometimes I'd win and sometimes I'd lose. We had a good time, but it was a good time because Jesus was there and some of these men came to see Jesus Christ as their Lord and Savior.

## CHAPTER SEVEN

## TIME

The native folks don't think of time as we white folks do. The clock is a white man's invention in their mind and they're not tied to it. One Sunday afternoon there was a special service at the Gakona Chapel. Gakona was a little village outside of Glennallen and that chapel was one of the first that Vince Joy, the founder of the central Alaskan mission, had started that became independent and self-supportive.

They had a native pastor at the time, Pastor Freddie Ewon. He was to lead a special service Sunday afternoon at 3 o'clock. To the natives, if you're going to meet at 3 o'clock, that means we'll start as soon after 3 o'clock as enough people get there to make it worth starting. They're not tied to that "when the big hand hits 12" concept.

So at 3 o'clock they looked around and all of the white folks, the missionaries, and people from Glennallen were in their seats patiently waiting or just waiting. About 25 after three there were enough native folks there to make it worth starting the service, so Pastor Ewon stepped up on the platform. Before he got behind the pulpit and turned to face the congregation, he reached up to the open-faced clock on the wall behind the pulpit and turned the hands back to 3 o'clock. Then he turned around and faced the congregation and said, "For our white brother, we'll start on time."

The natives don't get as bound up with time as we do. They look forward to eternity. They don't waste time, but they also aren't tied by time. They relax. Sometimes we lose sight of eternity because we're too busy looking at the clock. There are a lot of divine interruptions that God sends our way and we can't always be there at 3 o'clock straight up or at whatever the other appropriate time is because things happen. We need to find that people are more important than time. I thank the Lord that He taught me that concept through the native people.

This chapter has a special significance in that it happened the summer of 1989 when my mother and father, Reverend and Mrs. H.L. Pearce, visited me and they were present at that time. In all probability the white folks that Pastor Ewon was being respectful to were my parents.

## CHAPTER EIGHT

## A DAY IN THE LIFE OF A BUSH MISSIONARY

The mission I was working for had started out as a church planting mission and had grown into some other facets, Bible College, radio station, additional training, and a medical unit at the hospital. At the particular time I was based in Chistochina. I was the last missionary in the outlying areas of Alaska with the mission.

One winter a man who was going to work as a fundraiser for the mission came to Alaska. He was a public relations man. That was his profession. And he was hired by them. He wanted to see exactly what a missionary in the bush in Alaska did as a normal daily activity. So I had to drive down to Glennallen 50 miles and pick him up, bring him out to Gakona, show him one of the first chapels that had become independent and separated from the mission and became self-supporting and had a native pastor at some times; it didn't at that particular time.

Then I brought him up to Chistochina and I was to show him the work there, which was an ongoing work that the mission was still hoping would become independent and self-supporting at some point. It was a pleasant enough day, probably 15 or 20 below. It was not particularly cold for Alaska that time of year. We had snow on the ground, but the roads were clear. We had a pleasant trip, pleasant ride. He was a real fine fellow. He videotaped everything he saw, every place he went. He recorded and took notes because all this was his research.

As I pulled into the drive at Chistochina, we were going to give him soup and a sandwich and then show him that chapel and we were going on up the road to Slana to show him the work that had not been begun by the mission, but that the mission was assisting through our activities from Chistochina. We were hoping someday the two chapels would unite at least in spirit to help each other for social activities for support and all.

Anyway, I pulled in the drive. My wife came tearing out onto the porch with a cordless phone and she was obviously very excited. She handed me the phone. The neighbor, Bev Hermans, was on the phone. She was out of breath and all she could say was "dog fight, help." And instantly I recognized the clatter coming from their dog yard.

We had given them several dogs when my son and I quit running the team, and they needed exercise. We had given them several and they had a number of their own. They probably had 12 or 14 sled dogs.

I could hear the fight and I went running the shortest route, but it was through some fairly deep snow, so I was sort of plowing snow. I got there and Cesar, which had been one of our dogs, was the wheel dog, the big strong dog that pulled right close to the sled and actually helped the sled change direction according to what the lead dog would get him to do.

Cesar, probably 75 to 80 pounds, had Dancer, one of their dogs, down by the throat in the snow. There was blood everywhere. We had no idea how much damage there was. Dancer had gotten loose from his chain and had got into Cesar's territory. When he did, Cesar just attacked thinking that he was the emperor since he had that name. The last thing you want to do in a dog fight is stick your hand in the middle of it.

So I looked quick and I saw the shovel that Chuck used to clean up the dog yard and I grabbed it, whacked Cesar in the head, screamed his name "Cesar". I knew that he'd jump back with that because he'd have to get oriented and figure out what happened and from where. And as he jumped back, I grabbed his collar and slung him in the air. I was holding him about four feet off the ground. He couldn't bite me, couldn't do much of anything. Dancer was up and gone the split second that Cesar was off him.

As I turned and looked back, this fundraiser was busy videotaping, and I was wondering how this would go. *Bush missionary hits dogs in the head with shovel, hangs them by their collars*. Don't know how he ever used that in his fundraising. I never did see any of his work, but it was an interesting day.

For you dog lovers, the only blood had come from a tooth that Cesar had pulled loose in his efforts to hold Dancer down and there was no permanent or expensive damage to any of the animals.

## CHAPTER NINE

## MOOSE HUNTING IN ALASKA

Alaska requires you to be a resident for one full year before you're allowed to get a resident hunting license. For particular interest, it's a subsistence hunting license, which I did get my second year in Alaska.

The first year I did go out hunting, both for moose and caribou with some other guys. I didn't carry a rifle; I carried a pistol for my own protection in case I ran into a bear or something. I helped them pack meat and learned a little of the Alaskan style hunting and got a little more familiar with the area. I had some good times. Good times with fellowship in camp and in the evenings.

When the time came, I got my hunting license. I was ready to go moose hunting. The first day of season Bob Hamilton, who lived over on the Chistochina airport, became a real good friend. He's part Indian, but he's Cherokee not Athabascan. He'd come up from the lower 48 and sort of took me under his wing. He was a real good hunter, a good sportsman, good friend.

He had a CESSNA 170, which had not flown for a good many years. We got it back in the air and we had flown over the territory the day before looking things over and he spotted a pretty good size moose not too far from where I was actually living. You're not allowed to hunt the day that you fly, for obvious reasons.

So we waited the 24 hours until the time was up after we landed and we started out the first day of hunting season. I was carrying the Springfield 30-06 that my dad and I had sportorized when I was about 14 years old. And I was carrying some of Bob Roses' hand loads.

Bob was a sergeant in Richland County Sheriff's Department. When I left for Alaska he gave me some real potent hand loads, adequate for either stopping a bear or a moose or whatever.

But we set out and got to the area where we spotted that moose and were just about to take a break from our walk when Bob sort of hunkered down and pointed. I told him that I appreciated all of his kindness, but I understood the etiquette of hunting whoever sees it first gets the first shot at it. I expected him to go ahead and carry that out, and if he got a moose before I did I'd just help him pack his out and do my best. We'd probably take him back in to have him guide me anyway. He spotted this moose and he tried to get me to take a shot and I said, "No, it's your shot", pointing at him. Of course the rules are if a man takes a shot and doesn't hit it, then it's free game for whoever's next in line.

So he realized I wasn't going to take a shot until he did, so he shot the 300 Winchester Magnum just nowhere near the animal. He just got the shot off and sort of painted me into the corner, so I had to go ahead. And I had that thing in that six-power scope and when Bob fired, the moose bolted up the crest of a little hill and I realized that he was going to be out of sight in just seconds. And I led him about as much as I figured I could and squeezed off real fast. And in the scope I saw that moose just fold up.

We waited a little bit, eased on up there over the hill and couldn't find the moose. Of course over the hill there was a fairly good sized pond. There was tall grass in it, sort of like bull rushes. I don't know what they are in Alaska, but sort of like the bull rushes or cane of the southern country.

So I started floundering around looking and I realized that this moose had gone over the hill and straight into a lake. And if my guess was right and I had actually hit him, he probably crawled off or was down in those weeds. I took my rifle on my shoulder with the sling. We looked around and I laid my rifle down, let Bob watch it, and I started wading in the pond. The pond was probably two-and-a-half, three feet deep. I got out a ways and sure enough there was the moose as dead as a hammer all set out for cutting up, cleaning up, taking it home to eat. Hunting was sport, but it was also grocery shopping for us.

I could move him all over in the pond because he was floating, but as soon as I came to the bank we had a real steep bank, about seven, eight feet up, and we couldn't get him up the bank. Well, Bob being the true friend and sportsman and old guide that he was, jumped down in the water.

We had run into another friend of mine who had been a guide in times past. We hadn't started together, but we ran into him out there. He decided to help skin that moose out and cut it up. They skinned it out and cut it up in the water, and we just brought it up a piece at a time because we couldn't come up that bank carrying that much weight.

I didn't get a chance to skin my moose. I had two old-time guides with real sharp knives moving a lot faster than I was going to get my hand in the middle of. We helped pack it and got it up and brought it home.

The tradition is you get the fellows to pack and the one that goes to get the packers carries out the liver. It's about a four or five-pound liver in the moose. We'd always keep some good sweet onions during hunting season. The other missionary packed the liver out for me and got Frankie Charlie, a young friend from the chapel, and they came back and we packed it out and got it home.

When we got to the lodge Bob's sister, Terry, had cooked up the liver and onions for us. It was just absolutely delicious at the end of a hard day, a bunch of walking, a bunch of packing and carrying. Everybody was hungry, and the moose liver by itself is tender and tasty. I will say if you ever eat moose liver you won't care to eat cow's liver or calves' liver again. I've had to go down to venison. I do like that kind of meat but it's not available. You can't get moose liver down here in the south.

The moose was only about 900 pounds, somewhere in there and had a 30-inch rack, which is not big. He was just two-and-a-half, three years old.

The interesting thing was as they cut this animal up I was looking to find out where the bullet was, number one, to get the bullet out of the way so nobody ends up biting down on it when it's cooked; and number two, just to evaluate how good a shot the guy was. Well, they went through the whole thing. They cut that up, packed it out and over the period of the next 18 months to two years we ate it all up. We never did find the bullet, the bullet hole, or any blood.

Now, I said that I missed it so close I scared it to death, but Bob said I missed it so far away he died laughing at me. I don't know what the story was, but it was good eating. It was the only moose I got during my three years in Alaska. It was a good experience with a good friend, a number of good friends really. The hunting helps to bond men together. And being involved in hunting and airplanes and trapping with the men helped to build relationships that God honored in bringing men into the chapel.

## CHAPTER TEN

## JAMES 5:14

James 5:14 says that if any man is sick he needs to call for the elders of the church, have them anoint him with oil, pray for him, and God says he will heal the sick.

Sometimes people in the bush in Alaska find God is so real because they don't have anything else. I have a t-shirt that says Jesus on the front and on the back it says, "You'll probably never know Jesus is all you need until Jesus is all you have." Many of those people in the bush in Alaska literally have no resources other than God.

Many people in the Slana area, the Homestead Village, have a small portable generator, at least two or three horsepower, probably 2.5 kilowatt. It runs on a gas/oil mixture, a little two-cycle engine. And at 6 o'clock in the evening in the winter time they crank up their generators and turn on their little 8 to 10 or 12-inch portable TV and watch the Rat Net. That's rural Alaska television. I always thought it may have to do more with the quality of the programming than anything else, as they called it the Rat Net.

But anyway, these people would watch the news, and then when the news went off at 6:30 they'd plug in their CB radio and they'd communicate with the other people within range, just sort of a social time. Most people didn't have cars, or if they did have a car, they didn't have a way to get it started in the winter time, and it was 50 below, so they were pretty much limited. That was their social contact for sometimes several days, or a week when the weather was real cold.

There was one occasion when a lady brought her generator in from outside and put it next to a wood stove, brought the glass jar, the mixture of gas and oil inside and let it warm up so that she could start it. She was busy doing things, but then it started to warm up. She had a grandson who stayed with her who had some severe mental restrictions. He got a hold of the bottle of gas/oil and drank it, nearly a quart from what they said. She was obviously distressed.

She's 160 miles from a hospital, 35 miles from the nearest medical advice of any kind other than Wanda. Wanda was the church treasurer and church secretary in Slana. She'd been a nursing assistant in Seattle before she had come to Slana and so she had a little bit of medical knowledge. She was a very wise lady and met many of the emergency needs on a regular basis, just as an opportunity to witness for the Lord.

The lady who had the disaster managed to get the generator cranked up, got the CB going, and got Wanda on the CB and told her the situation and told her she needed help. Wanda put on her parka and her snow shoes and trudged through the snow probably a mile to get there. And, of course, there's already a good time that had elapsed by the time this has all happened. She came in and she really had no medical knowledge of how to treat this with anything that she had available. She looked at the lady and said, "James 5:14 says we're to anoint him with oil and pray for him and God will heal him."

The other lady said to Wanda, "It says the elders are supposed to do that and we don't even have a man in the church." Wanda looked at her and said, "We must be the elders then." She took a little salad oil and anointed that boy and laid her hands on him and prayed. Her testimony is, the boy burped, sat up, and walked around the cabin as if nothing had ever happened.

Isn't it wonderful when people can just believe God's word and trust Him totally and watch His word work in their lives and the lives of the people they touch? I trust that that would be your experience. There are many, many scriptures that tell us to trust God's care, His protection, His presence and promise that He will be sufficient in all our needs.

Read the Bible. It's a good place to start.

## CHAPTER ELEVEN

## WHAT ARE YOU WORTH?

An old guide told me they never get involved in conversations with the clients about religion or politics or money. Those things you just stayed away from. If it upset the clients, they were liable to go find another guide in future years and they stayed away from those controversial subjects.

A guide related a story to me about three men who came to Alaska regularly. They graduated from high school together and they sort of had a reunion every year or so in Alaska for a sheep hunt. They were getting up in age a little bit. He had known them many years and enjoyed guiding them and he always took them himself. He had other guides to guide other customers.

But around the campfire one time one of the guys said to them, "I finally made it; I'm worth a million dollars this year." And the second guy says, "Well, I'm worth at least two and a half million. The third guy sort of snickered and said, "Anybody who knows what he's worth ain't worth much." So the guide stayed out of the conversation and just let it pass and they went on and did their hunt and went on back to their respective homes.

The next year they came back about the same time, late August, early September, and this guide took them out again and set them up for a nice sheep hunt. Around the campfire they were talking and the one guy says, "Well, things are going better. I'm worth about a million and a half this year, had a real good year. The second guy says, "Well, I'm worth about 4 million. And the third guy said, "I'm worth 17.5 million."

At that point the guide said he just couldn't resist it. He jumped in and said, "Hey, what's this business? Anybody who knows what he's worth ain't worth nothing." The guy said, "It was easy, my wife's attorney added it up and divided it by two."

What are you worth? I'm probably not going to be listed on Dunn and Bradstreet on any of those important financial documents. Jesus said, "Lay not up for yourselves treasures on earth where moth and rust does corrupt and where thieves break through and steal, but lay up for yourselves treasures in heaven."

Where's your treasure? Are you worth 17.5 million? Are you worth a nickel? All of the treasures of heaven come by God's grace. God has provided a way where a man who's too poor to pay for a phone call needs only to bow his heart before Almighty God in turn asking Jesus Christ into his life in order to have treasures in heaven that can't be taken away by a divorce attorney or a thief. They won't rust, they won't corrupt. Seek ye first the kingdom of God and His righteousness and all these things will be added unto you.

## CHAPTER TWELVE

## CESSNA 170

Bob Hamilton got to be a good friend. He's the guy who took me moose hunting when I got my moose and did a lot of things to help me around the chapel and the parsonage, especially with generator problems and was just a handy man and a good friend.

Sometime before I got there he'd bought a Cessna 170 at a real good price because it hadn't flown for a long time, hadn't been inspected, and hadn't started. There were no records on it and no log books. So the man just sold it to him "as is, where is". Bob never had any flying lessons, but he's great at operating any kind of equipment. He's just a genius with his hands and feet.

Bob called me one day and said, "Al, you've got the license, you can put this thing together and make it legal to fly, let's do it, and then you teach me to fly it." I said, "That sounds like a project because it's going to take some time, but I'll be glad to work with you on it."

We set a date and went out and looked it over and did a few things on it. We got the brakes fixed and checked it out and got it cranked up where we could run it. Bob asked what it would take to get it back in license. By that time we had pretty well figured it out. I told him to make it legal to fly we were going to have to either come up with the log books or reconstruct the log books to the best of our ability.  It was going to be a huge project paperwork wise.

I told him I'd be willing to do it.  He paid all of the expenses and I took the time to write to the FAA and got the various work orders and inspection reports and 337's, which are major modifications or repairs that had been done to it over the years.  We found out that the airplane had gone through three accidents, totally different causes for each one, but each ended the same way with the airplane flipped over on its back and the rudder, a wing, the cabin structure damaged each time.  All of those parts had been replaced three different times on that airplane.

We checked it out and worked on it and got it legal.  Lee Adler, another buddy of mine from Glennallen who was a gunsmith who sold and shipped guns, which generated a lot of interest, came up.  He had a lot of experience in tail wheel planes, which I didn't at that time.  He took it out for its maiden voyage for the first time in, I don't know, 10, 12, 14 years since it had flown.  He came back and said it was fine.  He let me get in the right seat and fly it from the right seat.  He sat in the left seat to keep me from hurting myself until I got used to it.

I got comfortable enough in it that I told Bob it was time.  Bob got in and strapped that thing on. Bob was a good bit taller than me.  If I sat where I could reach the rudder pedals, he sat about four inches behind me and I had to sort of look over my shoulder to talk to him.  The airplane had been stripped out in times past.  There wasn't any insulation, so you could hear every noise on the inside.  It was hard to talk.

We started teaching. We had a good time learning to fly. I was learning to teach in a tail wheel. We were able to get it up and around.

There was an occasion when I needed to go to Glennallen to get a part for the heater for the house real quick because it was cold and things were going to freeze if I didn't get it. It was about a two hour and 15 minute round-trip for me to drive down there and go to the place and pick it up and get back. We could fly down there in about 20 minutes. I had a guy meet us at the airport with the parts, so just an hour into the project we were getting heat back in the house before it froze.

We did have some fun. We would fly and spot game just for fun. That's the airplane we flew when we spotted the moose that I got the first year I hunted in Alaska. Bob was again the man who took me moose hunting.

But over the years Bob added some things, put some larger tires on it and made it more like a bush plane, and in the winter time put some skis on it. That was the only airplane that I ever instructed in on skis. I had a lot of fun, but I think as the instructor I learned more than the student did.

Bob wasn't able to get his license before I left Alaska, for a number of reasons, but we parted as good friends and I still think the world of him. I don't know what happened to the 170. I haven't been to Alaska to find out. If I catch up with it again I'll let you know.

## THIRTEEN

# ALASKA AIR MAIL

One of the things about the airplane competitions which the bush pilots held time and again at different airports, everybody's proud of how quickly you can get an airplane off the ground. Of course, a lot of times they're flying off of roads and tundra and sandbars, depending on what they're doing, guiding for fishing or hunting. I missed a spot landing contest trying to put an airplane down within inches of the mark, and some of these bush pilots can really do it.

But one of the other forms of competition is called the "bomb drop". They drop little paper bags full of flour at the Gakona airport fly-in. They always used the outhouse as the target and they hit circles around the target out to about 40 feet. And if you were more than 40 feet off the mark you weren't even in the competition with those folks. But I saw one guy drop and nobody saw any flour. I mean, they saw the bag coming down and then just lost sight of it and there wasn't any puff from the flour when the bag burst. The scorekeeper ran up and pulled open the outhouse door and out poured the smoke. He had hit it straight down the vent tube of the outhouse. It was probably about a six or eight-inch pipe.

That competition has a purpose. It's cute to be able to drop something from an airplane and get it at a given mark, but the purpose for that and the reason that competition started was a lot of times bush pilots can't land directly at a place. Say, for instance, they're flying supplies in to someone who has a cabin up in the woods away from the river where they could land on a sandbar or maybe in a float plane to bring in supplies, but they need to get communications to them for various reasons.

Of course, whenever you're doing business you've got to be able to communicate and the Alaskans developed a way to get messages. They would write out their message and place it in some type of container and put a streamer on it and buzz the place to get attention. When the people came out they would drop the container and, of course, with the streamer on it they could see it, and they'd run to get it and pull out the message. They had various responses to send a reply and it was a right important way of making communication.

One day Jim Hummell, who is the park ranger at Wrangell St. Elias National Park in Slana, called me. He had an old Stinson 108 dash 1; 150 horsepower, all fabric. He told me that he had gotten a message. There was a couple with a small baby canoeing in a green or orange canoe down the Gakona River and they had a family member who had been rushed to the hospital. They were needed at the hospital and we needed to get a message to them and he asked if I could help him. And I said, "Well, yeah, we'll do what we can." And with this description we started out.

We used the old Kool-Aid expanding jugs for message containers. We used to buy them in Alaska with the powdered Kool-Aid in them. They looked like a coiled spring. When you took the top off and pulled them open and added two quarts of water, put the lid on it and shook it up you had two quarts of Kool-Aid.

Well, these same things are real small to carry in an airplane. When they're folded down they're only a couple of inches tall. And when you unfold them, you've got a two-quart container so you can put in some items or a message or whatever and also they're big enough to find. We'd put on an orange streamer and just catch it inside the cap and screw the cap on and drop the message.

We only had two at that particular time, but we loaded the message with the family name and wrote, you've got an emergency; your relative has been taken to the hospital, and we gave the name of the hospital. We wrote that they needed to get to the nearest point, get out, and get there as quick as they could.

Jim had gotten when they started and where they started from, so his guess was they'd be coming near the confluence of the Gakona and the Copper. Of course, we were hoping to get them before they got to the Copper because that's flying in a different kind of territory. It's a steeper valley and it's going to be harder to pinpoint who's who.

But we started out and hadn't passed many markers beyond where Jim said he thought they could get in the time they had, when we spotted a canoe of the right color with two people in it and what looked like a baby in a baby carrier, which it really was.

We buzzed them several times until we had their attention and the fellow paddled over to a small island in the middle of the Gakona River and we dropped the first container. The poor guy, he knew we weren't professional bush pilots because we missed.  I hit it right dead into a thicket that he could probably never have gotten into.  But he wandered around trying to look and all, and then came back out in the open.  We got his attention and he looked up -- and keep in mind Alaskans are used to this.  When they get buzzed by an airplane they look for whatever is going to be dropped. As he stood there looking up at us we made the second drop.

We prayed, "Lord, you know we've only got two shots and this guy needs to get this message. We sure need your help." and dropped that one and it just about landed in his lap.  He pulled the top off, read the note, and waved thank you and hopped in that canoe and went paddling off downstream, as fast as he could.  So we knew he had gotten the message and understood what it was and we had the right party.

So that was one of the few times that I had the privilege of delivering Alaska airmail.  It was a good time with Jim Hummell, a good brother in the Lord. We had a Bible study in his home for a couple of years while I was there in Chistochina and Slana. God is good in accomplishing His purpose in helping somebody in a time of need.

Part of serving the Lord is trying to bring people to Him and bring them to salvation, but it's also caring about people's needs and helping with those needs.  We call it "lifestyle evangelism" because you had to show them you cared and you love them before they'd even listen to you tell them. For the natives it is so true that 'what you do speaks so loud I can't hear what you say'.

## CHAPTER FOURTEEN

## NOTHING WASTED

I had been in Chistochina a little while, probably a year, when a guy named Rudy Merrick stopped by and asked if he could stay the night. Rudy is from Banks, Oregon. He had written a book called *North to Alaska, the Studebaker Story*, about a trip he had made in a Studebaker up the ALCAN Highway in the early '50s. Then he decided to redo that trip after he was older and retired. He was a former cop and traveling evangelist doing tract and Bible distribution, all entirely with his own funds. He was not with any organization.

Anyway, Rudy stopped by and it was the first time I met him. We got to talking and he asked about my background. I told him I had been a cop for fifteen years at that time and I was a pilot and an airplane mechanic. I had done quite a few different things over the years to make a living and to accomplish things. The Lord had been good to me, given me a lot of chances to expand my areas of exposure.

Old Bob Hamilton came up and we were talking and Bob said, "You know, it's a shame to waste all of the stuff that you've learned, all of the experience that you've had up here where there's very few people." And I thought a minute and I said, "You know, Bob, I haven't wasted anything. I've used every experience I've ever had. And then I paused and for some reason I thought about my college days in Columbia Bible College in '70 through '73. I had worked repairing and rebuilding fire extinguishers and it just struck me that I hadn't done anything with fire extinguishers since I had been in Alaska. And I laughed and I said, "Well, just one thing, building fire extinguishers. And he laughed. He said, "Yeah, there's probably not a market for that around here."

But we went on and had a good visit. Rudy left and that weekend we had the Covenant Four Quartet fly in to Chistochina. We had a special hymn sing at the chapel and they gave a concert. They flew in in two planes with all their sound equipment and everything and had a great time.

Because of that great time and because they were well known throughout Alaska, we had a pretty good response. We had 45 or 50 people in our little chapel that Friday night. During the concert a person slipped in and tapped Bob Hamilton on the shoulder. Bob was the fellow I had told that the only thing I wasted was fire extinguisher filling. He went outside with him and I heard his truck pull away. And then just a minute later that person came back in and said the Boston's house was on fire, they need help fighting the fire. Of course, there's no fire department out in rural Alaska. It's pretty much a volunteer thing. The state had dispersed a whole lot of dry chemical fire extinguishers and the equipment to refill it, but they never trained anybody how to do it, so it was a one-shot deal.

We got up there and the log home was what the firemen would call "fully involved". It didn't look like there was any hope of saving anything. Half of the roof had caved in and the other half was burning. Bob was the nearest thing we had to a fire chief and he was pretty good at organization. He wanted a minute to get down there and organize things in his own mind so that he could use whatever resources we had.

Well, as Jon would say, it just so happened that the four guys of the Covenant Four Quartet had all been volunteer firemen and they had someone with them who was also a volunteer fireman. So we had six people who really had some experience and knew something. We were fighting it with garden hoses and dry chemical fire extinguishers. And, of course, after everybody shot them off we got all the buckets to refill them and nobody knew how to do it.

Here I was in the front yard of a burning log cabin directing people how to clean the valve, make sure it would seal, fill the fire extinguisher to the proper height so you would have room to get the air in there to charge it and then charging them off of an air bottle and passing them. The guys would run up there and hit a hot spot with their fire extinguisher and run back and we'd do it again. So I really got a kick out of the fact that less than 72 hours after I said that was the only thing I wasted here I was dead in the middle of it, not only doing it but teaching it to others.

And by God's grace we were able to save a good portion of that house. They rebuilt the other half, but we were able to save over half of the house. Just another thing about God, He's got a sense of humor. Right about the time you laugh and say, oh, I'll never use that again He says, oh. And he writes a program that puts you dead in the middle of using that. God was good. We had a lot of fun using the different talents in Alaska. I had a wonderful time with people. I was just amazed at the way that God would bring things together. We had never had a concert on Friday night. We had never had the Covenant Four Quartet.

Normally on a Friday night Chistochina is about abandoned because everybody went to other villages where something was happening. But it just so happened God had them call us and say, hey, can we come. And they said can we come and give a concert; they didn't say, can we come and help fight your fires, but that's what they ended up doing. God is great, God is good. He orchestrates it all in such a wonderful way that nothing is wasted.

# CHAPTER FIFTEEN

## HOMESTEAD PROPERTY LINE

The village of Slana, Alaska was a homestead village. The government decided they would allow people to move in there, live on their chosen piece of property for nine months out of the year for five years out of seven and add improvements on the property, which could be anything from a tent to a mobile home. When they had completed all the requirements there would be a survey and then the deed would be recorded and the property would be deeded over to them.

Well, a whole bunch of people went to Alaska thinking they were going to get something and the government just really wasn't too nice about that. Slana was almost a swamp. It had no road structure within it, and it wasn't well defined. Some people were way outside of the homestead proper, but it was up in the mountains and nobody cared, so the government ended up giving them a deed if they met the requirements.

On Nebesna Road a fellow moved into a little 8-foot by 26 or 28-foot home and started his homestead. He had gone off somewhere, came back and some fellows were building a place next door to him. They built an outhouse on what he thought was his property line. Not wanting to disturb anything that was theirs, but not wanting them on his place, when they were gone that evening he cut the outhouse in half and burned the half that was on his property. Of course, none of these property lines are defined, so it's all real subjective.

Anyway, as he thought about it, there were a couple of them and one of him and he decided maybe he had better not be at home when they came back and found out they had half an outhouse. So he took off somewhere and stayed a couple days.

Well, the fellows came home and they saw the outhouse and they realized from the way it was cut and burned what the problem was, so they went over and visited the little mobile home. And when the guy came back several days later his 8-foot by 26-foot mobile home was cut in half long ways with a chainsaw.

At the time I left that place was still sitting the same way. He moved off. He decided not to try to homestead and he never did move the mobile home. It sort of deteriorated and became a landmark that everybody would laugh about, right at the end of the road going up to Devils Mountain up Nebesna Road.

## SIXTEEN

## A DIVINE INTERRUPTION

The stories in this book are told to illustrate the goodness of God and His mercy and His grace and how He works in all circumstances of life to accomplish the good of His people. One of the stories in this book tells of a time when a man called on me to help him just before the service and I couldn't get to the service on time if I did so I sent him somewhere else. God convicted me of that and worked to show me that His plan was best and that when someone who needed me crossed my path I needed to be willing to let Him, and others who were there, take care of the church.

Chistochina and Slana were 28 miles apart and this happened on the road to Slana in the winter of 1990. I preached at the Chistochina Chapel on Sunday morning at 11 o'clock and then at the Slana Homestead Christian Church, which we just called the Slana Chapel, at three in the afternoon. Slana Chapel had no electricity and the heat was just a wood stove. Some of the folks in town would get there a little early and get a fire going and warm up the building. Slana is on what is traditionally called Four-Mile Road, which was not much more than a series of ruts at the time I was there, and you had to ford the creek since there was no bridge.

It was cold, probably 35 below. Everything was frozen up solid, but there was a very powerful spring just above the place where we forded the creek. It would push up through the ice and cause what they called overflow. Water was flowing on several feet of thick ice. You could drive across the ice, but the water flowing across it made it impossible to walk across. As soon as you stop the flow of water at that temperature the water would freeze. If you were unfortunate enough to fall in there, hypothermia would set in in seconds.

I came up to that spot where I had to ford in my little S-10 Chevy pickup four-wheel drive and I saw off to the side, downstream a little bit, a fellow named Jimmy who had an S-10 pickup just about the same as mine. It was also four-wheel drive. He had started to ford the creek and the overflow had pushed him downstream. Jimmy was notorious for not being prepared to drive and maybe drinking a little too much. I stopped and got out and called to him, made sure that he was all right. He said he was. I asked him if he had a tow strap and he said, yeah. And he did have a tow strap that he kept hooked to the rear bumper of his truck because he got in so many spots to get towed out of that he just laid the tow strap back up in the bed.

So he crawled out the window and back into the bed of the truck and got the tow strap. He tossed the loose end up to me and I hooked it to the front bumper of my pickup. We coordinated and got them both going, both four-wheel drives engaged and we were able to get him out of the little hollow he was in and back up on the road.

We got out and unhooked the tow strap and Jimmy looked at me and said, 'When does your service start?" I said, "Oh, about 3 o'clock." And he looked at his watch and he said, "Well, you're late." I said, "Well, Jimmy, I'm exactly where God wants me because He loves you every bit as much as anybody that comes into church and you needed me and I'm glad to help you. I appreciate your taking note of that, but I didn't want to put the church ahead of you and God doesn't put the church ahead of you."

It got a little awkward. He wasn't too comfortable with the preaching, so he said he had to go. So we got in and I got across the overflow okay and he turned around and went on out of the village.

I got up to the chapel and they had already started and everything was going fine. As time went on, time and again, after the service started when nobody could catch him, Jimmy would sneak in the back door. In Slana people came and went just pretty much independently, so you were never rude and looked to see who came in or who left when the door opened. You just concentrated on the service and tried not to embarrass anybody. But he would sneak in and listen to my message and he would hear me preach, and then during the closing prayer he would sneak out. He was not unfriendly to the church people but it was just awkward for him and he didn't know exactly how to be comfortable around them.

Well, as time went on the Slana Chapel burned to the ground one Saturday. Chuck Hermans, who was my neighbor there in Chisto, and I were outside talking. Chuck was scheduled to preach in the Chistochina Chapel the next morning and he had sent the message on the Caribou Clatters, which is a public announcement radio station, to invite everybody in the valley to come to Chistochina and hear him preach his first sermon.

We were standing there talking and a kid on a motorcycle came up and screamed "The Slana church is burning, the Slana church is burning we need help." Well, I got in the old Mercury. I had a '78 Mercury Cougar and that thing would run and it would stay on the road pretty well. At a time like that speed limits really don't mean much. It was a winding, curvy road, up and down hill. Chuck was behind me in a Ford F-250 diesel pickup and there were a couple of times I didn't touch the brakes because if I did he was going to hit me. He pushed that thing so hard.

We got there and the nearest water source to Slana was several miles from the church, so carrying enough buckets to stop an 80-foot by 40-foot building from burning was just really not practical. People were trying to save what they could, but the fire had gotten too hot and they were out of the building. We got there in time to see the bell frame burn through and the big bell come crashing down through the floor.

It was a traumatic moment in the life of all those people, even those who didn't attend the chapel in Slana. It was a landmark and was special in a lot of respects. They would use it for community meetings, but also that bell, which was just hung by a rope inside the door, could be used to call the village in time of need. And usually if there was a fire or anything somebody would get to the chapel and ring that bell to get everybody's attention and get them in gear to do whatever needed done.

Well, this was a hard time. Up until that point the Slana Chapel and the Chistochina Chapel had not done anything together with any regularity. We hoped that the two would somehow join as sister churches and get involved together in projects and in encouraging each other and helping each other to grow, but the cultures were greatly different. Homestead was primarily white folks who had come from the lower 48, and the Chistochina village was native and whites mixed, but most of the whites who lived in Chistochina were related to natives either by marriage or their children's marriage.

Though Chuck was there to try and help, once the building was burning there wasn't a whole lot that could be done to save it. When the threat was over, we headed back to Chistochina after we had prayed with the people that God's grace would intervene and that someday there would be a chapel there again.

Well, the next day they came to Chistochina because they didn't have a church to go to. Chuck preached, and it was ironic because he preached on the passage in James that says if you take special note and make special provisions for the rich man and push the poor man aside, you're really not honoring God. For his first message he preached for 47 minutes, which is really long for a first sermon, but it was so appropriate. The people of Chistochina were much better off financially than the people in Slana for the most part.

We had a potluck after the service and we ate together and, of course, entertained Slana people as our guests. After we were finished cleaning up, the people of Slana said we want to go back to our church, to the spot where it was, and pray together and dedicate that ground towards having a chapel there again.

Chuck and several others went with me that time, and that truly was a day of firsts. The morning service was Chuck's preaching at Chistochina and then the afternoon is when we had a service at the site that was still smoldering ruins.

Little Wanda, who was the treasurer of the Slana Chapel, said, "God promised the oil of joys of mourning and beauty for ashes." She reached down and picked up a handful of those warm ashes and threw them in the air and said, "I'm claiming God's promise that there will be a church here again."

That was a neat day, a really special time. As the Lord would have it, before the Slana Chapel got rebuilt, I came back to the lower 48, back to South Carolina. I kept in touch with them and from now on the things I tell you about were related to me by people through phone calls and letters and later on some e-mails.

They raised some funds to buy the supplies to rebuild the chapel and had a work crew who was coming up after the spring breakup, probably around March. But they had to have the permit signed and in place so the work crew would not be frustrated by coming a thousand miles from home to do a job they couldn't do.

They figured out when the deadline was and Wanda and Alice got their walking boots on and walked over to Jimmy's house. Jimmy was on a pension and a lot better off than most. He had a generator and he actually had a heated garage, so he could run his car all year round without a whole lot of problems.

They walked over there and asked him if he would give them a ride to the Bureau of Land

Management, the BLM office, to get the permit to rebuild the chapel since none of their cars were running at the time. And he said sure he'd be glad to do that. Jimmy was always very cordial with the people from the church.

So they headed out for Glennallen, went down there on the Richardson Highway and pulled into the Bureau of Land Management office. When it's 40 or 50 below you don't sit and wait in the car, so Jimmy got out and walked in, but they sort of stayed aloof from him.

He walked around reading things on the wall and just sort of acted nonchalant. Wanda and Alice went up and told the clerk why they were there and said they wanted the permit to rebuild the Slana Chapel. The clerk checked some things and said, "You can't have a church there, that's government property and, you know, separation of church and state, you can't put a church there." They tried to explain to him that the church had always been there until it burned and now they had a work crew coming and they had the materials and they just needed this permit to put it right back where it had been.

The guy got a little bit more adamant, "You can't have a church on government property and you're not going to build anything related to religion on that piece of property." Well, all of a sudden Jimmy got rambunctious and he said come on, come on, we've got to go, let's go. And, of course, if you're 150 miles from home and it's 40 below you go when the driver wants to go, you don't take any chance on walking home.

So they got in the car. They were terribly frustrated and couldn't understand what was going on. They knew they had to have the permit in the next week or so to satisfy the requirements of that work crew, but they got in the car and headed down the road. Jimmy, instead of going up the Richardson Highway to the cutoff and heading towards Slana, turned into the Glenn Highway, went down into Glennallen and took them to the Caribou restaurant and bought them lunch.

Well, they were a little confused, but always thankful for a good well-cooked meal that somebody else pays for. He ordered their lunch and took care of the bill, but he didn't stop to eat with them. He went out to the pay phone. He was on the pay phone for a while. They were getting along with their lunch, but hadn't finished yet. Jimmy came back, come on, come on, we got to go; we got to go.

And so they got to-go boxes and put what was left of their lunch in there and got into his car and they started up the road and Wanda said, "Where are we going? He said, "We're going to the Bureau of Land Management." Wanda said, "We just got thrown out of there." He laughed and just went on.

They pulled up; they all got out and walked in. The clerk who had been so adamant that they couldn't have a chapel there was standing there waiting. He had the papers all filled out. He told them to just sign here. And they signed and they got their paperwork and thanked the man and they left with their permit.

They were going up the road and Wanda said she waited just a little while because Jimmy wasn't a real talkative guy anyway, but she said, "Jimmy, what just happened?" And Jimmy said, "You know that stuff they've got on the walls, the president of the United States and the vice president of the United States and all of this stuff?" "Yeah." "And they had the secretary of the Bureau of Land Management?" "Yeah." He said, "I'm a disabled vet from Viet Nam and the secretary of the Bureau of Land Management was my company commander in Viet Nam and I saved his life over there in combat. He told me if you ever need me for anything you just call me." He said, "When I recognized his name and realized it was him, I just went down and called him." He, of course, took charge and they got the permit for the chapel.

The chapel was rebuilt and I just recently got pictures of it. It's a beautiful little building dedicated to the Lord. Jimmy started coming to the chapel after he was involved in rebuilding it or getting the permit to rebuild it. Jimmy was actually saved in that little chapel. He accepted Jesus Christ as his Savior just shortly before he died.

I'll see Jimmy again because he's now a brother in Christ. I'm still thankful for God's grace. You see, people talk all about grace and how God does this and how God does that. God's grace is where He takes a sinner who doesn't even know Him yet, allows him to be instrumental in building the church so that he can come to church and meet Jesus Christ as his Savior.

I hope you've had some divine interruptions in your life. Schedules are wonderful, I work on them all the time, but those little things that God plugs in that are just not on the schedule often turn out to be the most rewarding. I don't know if Jimmy considered it a divine interruption in his life when we were able to get him out of the overflow, but I sure did and I'm so thankful that God is faithful to use anyone who is willing to serve Him and oftentimes even before they come to know the Savior. He uses their experiences to draw them to Himself.

## CHAPTER SEVENTEEN

# CHEECHACO

Cheechaco is another Athabascan word that you hear occasionally. If a white man asks a native what it means, he'll tell you it means little one. As they get to know you better they'll tell you more about that.

They called me to Cheechaco the first year in Chistochina and some of the white folks told me that I'd be a Cheechaco until I lived through 50 below one winter. That would probably cause them to drop that name. They tried to help me. They told me different things and particularly how to dress for the weather.

I read catalogs, you know. I knew how it should be done. I got myself a nice pair of these boots with a felt liner. You take the liners out and dry them out and you've got an extra pair of liners so that if the liner gets wet and you don't have time to dry it out you just put the other set in and you can wear them the rest of the day.

The natives told me they were good to about 30 below, but if it got colder than that I needed to get bunny boots. Jack Justin called them man killers. I asked him why he said that and he said, put them on and walk a few miles and you'll see.

Bunny boots are usually Air Force surplus. They're the white boots, big, bulky and they're insulated by air that surrounds your foot. It's sort of like a balloon inside of the boot. You actually could let the air out a little valve in the back if things got too warm and the pressure built up and the boot wasn't comfortable. Bunny boots were about $35 and I wasn't particularly well off and I thought, well, my pretty boots are probably going to be good enough for one winter anyway.

Well, I broke down. The old '78 Mercury Cougar broke down and I was standing in a snow drift alongside the road trying to get it functioning again. I found out that another of my brilliant Cheechaco ideas didn't work. I had gotten a hold of some pure antifreeze and I thought, well, pure antifreeze will cover everything you need in Alaska. And so rather than diluting it with water, and it was not the pre-diluted kind it was concentrated antifreeze, I put pure antifreeze in. Well, it got down to about 35, 40 below and without that liquid being diluted, it turned to sludge and it wouldn't go through the water pump and the car overheated. I had a mess on my hands.

But while I was standing there deciphering what the problem was in my nice pretty catalog ordered boots I froze my feet. By the time I got back to the house I had no feeling in my feet. One of my boys pulled my boot off and my foot fell and hit the floor and it sounded like a baseball bat. I didn't feel a thing. My feet were probably nearly frozen solid. I had some of the signs of frostbite and hyperthermia, but God was good, they warmed up and I had no permanent damage.

Immediately after that event I got the antifreeze in the car diluted and got it mixed 50/50 like you're supposed to do. I headed down to Glennallen to a missionary friend who had a pair of bunny boots for sale and bought the bunny boots.

The next time they saw me I was walking in bunny boots.

Jerry Charlie, the chief of Chistochina, became a dear friend. He's a fine man and just a delightful guy to have as the representative of the village. He laughed at me and said, "No more Cheechaco?" I asked him, "Jerry, what does Cheechaco really mean?" He said, "Well, we're polite. We tell you it means little one, but in reality it means babe in arms, helpless one. It's for poor people who don't know how to take care of themselves in Alaska."

The Lord was good to me. He took care of me and He provided many precious friends who shared their experience, their wisdom, their insights, and their equipment. I was able to function. And so after just one experience with hyperthermia and one experience of buying the right kind of boots and getting my car fixed up, they quit calling me Cheechaco.

## CHAPTER EIGHTTEEN

## THE SNAKE HUNT

I've already told you about the lion hunt in Alaska, but we also had a snake hunt in Alaska. Which is interesting because just as there are no lions in Alaska, there are no snakes in Alaska except a pet boa constrictor that got away from somebody. And of all places it got in the drain and came up out of the big storm drain at the airplane wash at Merrill Field in Anchorage.

Now, the airplane wash is primarily used by bush pilots and such that don't have access to a regular airport to wash planes. It's sort of like a coin operated thing, like a car wash. One thing you've got to know about bush pilots, besides being half crazy, they're always armed. They've got something that will spit fire and lead. They're carrying a pistol of some kind if they're moving anywhere near the airplane.

When this boa constrictor came up and slithered out of that drain, a number of bush pilots cut loose with what they had and killed that snake. They killed it real good. They actually ground it up almost into hamburger. It was laying there on the pavement. Again, the old problem of ricochets off the pavement, the bullets ricocheted and busted all the windows in the bank across the street.

Well, the people in the bank across the street got a little excited because when bullets started coming in the windows it just wasn't a normal situation. They called the Anchorage police who came over and immediately discovered the snake and all the bush pilots hanging around it.  They verified that nobody else was shooting at the bank on purpose.  They went over to the bank and got the information over there.  The people in charge of the bank told them the windows were going to cost about $5,000.

So the officer came back and addressed the group and told them the windows that just got shot out are going to be about $5,000 and somebody's got to pay.  One old gentleman took out a matchbook, wrote an account number on the inside of the matchbook and gave it to the police officer. He said, take that back to the lady at the bank, and he gave the lady's name, and said, she knows me, just tell her to take it out of that account.

So the snake got killed.  The bush pilots got cleared of any criminal activity, and the bank got paid for their windows.

## CHAPTER NINETEEN

## DON

A disabled fellow named Don in the homestead village in Slana had come to Alaska from Washington because he could do better up there on his disability. You could survive in Alaska with very limited funds if you were able to grow some vegetables in the summer time and do a little hunting in the winter time and can some salmon. It was always sort of a dream of his, though he planned to go when he was healthier and able to do more.

He had one of the best gardens in Slana and actually put together a hot house and was able to grow vegetables longer than most folks just because of his knowledge and wisdom with the greenhouse. He was a unique fellow. He was a very good, kind hearted man. He loved the Lord, but had problems with organized religion and the standard church. He had no real good relationships with missionaries who had tried to come into Slana before, for whatever reason. But I was blessed in getting to know him as a friend and that's basically what this story is about.

We needed a place to meet for a Bible study in Slana. His wife was very open for us to do that at their place, but she felt it was my place to ask him and let him say yes or no. She very much respected him as head of the house, but I hadn't met him yet. I went down to the cabin to meet him, and he was sitting down weeding his garden. Because of his back injury he couldn't bend over real well. What he would do was just sort of drag himself along, scoot along and weed the garden.

He had plenty of vegetables and gave many away and was very generous to others, particularly to any special needs. So when I met him I just sat down across the row from him and started pulling weeds and talking. We had a neat time. By the time we got to the end of the row he said it was time to quit for the day and I could come in and have a cup of coffee. Of course, I told him I didn't drink coffee; that I pretty much stayed on water, but he said he had plenty of that.

We went in and sat and talked a while and got acquainted and had a real good time.
I told him we were looking for a place in the homestead village to have a Bible study during the week. His response was, "If I can sit by my fire, by my stove, in my house, and I can just ease on out when I need to go out to my outhouse and not have to go traveling elsewhere I'd love to be involved in a Bible study and you-all will be welcome here."

As it developed, we had many good days, a lot of good times in the Bible study there in Slana in Don and Wanda's house. They're special people. I still hear from Wanda. Don has gone home to be with the Lord now. He struggled with many medical problems.

They took him into the hospital; I believe it was in Anchorage, after I left. Wanda reported to me just some of the story. She said he was fairly lucid and he asked to hold her hand and just wanted to recite the Lord's Prayer together. He did that and then he just eased back and went to sleep and went to be with Jesus.

I miss him, even though I haven't been around that area in a long time. I miss the encouragement that he was, the special way he would do things, the way he loved God and the way he loved people. I thank God for Don.

## CHAPTER TWENTY

## A BAD EXAMPLE

Whenever you're in ministry or in public service--and I've seen both as a pastor/missionary and also as a cop--there are people whose lives you may influence even though they never become directly involved in your field of duty. They're just sort of on the periphery. Sometimes you get a chance to minister to them; sometimes they're just sort of a casual influence and you hope and pray for them if they're involved in some way with some of your people.

That was the case with one of the fellows in the Homestead Village. He was a good fellow, he knew the Lord, but just didn't want to give up some old friends. He was married to a real fine lady who loved him and loved the Lord and the church. They had two little boys. She tried and tried to get him to come to church with her and he would drop in occasionally, but he wouldn't be regular and wouldn't really get involved in the church.

I was on the outside one time, (when you're in Alaska the outside is anyplace outside the borders of Alaska) having delivered an airplane for a friend down to Columbia, South Carolina. I had just gotten back and she asked me if I would please talk to him because there were some problems. .

To make a long story short, the man had gone out on an ice fishing trip with some pretty rough characters that he had hung around with for years. They had taken a good supply of liquid refreshment and had got to drinking and carrying on and one thing led to another and somehow – nobody's real clear on how it happened – the fellow got stabbed in the back and was seriously injured.

Wanda, who was the only medical person in Homestead village, had managed to pull him together and sewed him up with fishing line because that's all she had to work with at the time. She got the bleeding stopped and got him comfortable and he had started to heal by the time I got back.

His wife asked me if I would go by and speak with him that afternoon after church, actually in the evening hours so the boys would be in bed and I could talk with him more freely. I got there and the boys were still up even though it was fairly late so I asked him to take a ride with me. He was always willing to help me.

We took a ride to the end of Homestead Road and turned around at the end and I asked him in my usual gentle fashion, I need your help. He said, "Oh, yes, whatever I can do for you preacher." I said, "I need you to tell me what you want me to tell your boys and your widow when you get killed with this kind of foolishness." He looked at me in sort of disbelief. Perhaps the direct approach wasn't the best at the time, but I had his attention.

He replied that he wanted his boys in the church and his wife in the church and he wasn't interfering with them. I said," Well, that's true, but if you want your boys in the church when they're 15 years old, you're going to have to take them to church now. You can't send them and expect that when they become teenagers and they're able to make some decisions and some evaluations on their own that they will keep coming and think it's important if you don't think it's important enough to go now."

The fellow did get on with his relationship with God and was a good father. I haven't followed up. I haven't heard anything from him since I left Alaska. I don't know how he's doing, but I hope and pray that things are going well.

We all influence people. Sometimes it's our kids, sometimes it's our parents, sometimes it's our friends, but other times it's just people in the area that happen to watch us and what we do tells them where our priorities really are. Don't try and tell somebody you really love Jesus Christ if you're not involved in any of the things that He would be involved in.

We don't work towards salvation, but the apostle James tells us that if we have a relationship with God, we'll work. That relationship will cause us to actually do the good works that our heavenly Father wants in our lives to honor Him and to bring others to Him.

Are you a good example or a bad example? Everybody's an example one way or the other. Be an example for Christ or for, well, the devil, it's your choice.

## CHAPTER TWENTY-ONE

# POTLATCH

Most folks involved in churches, particularly Baptist churches in the south, are very familiar with a potluck. It's a dinner where everyone brings their favorite dish or their special dish, as it may be, and you take your chances on what shows up. But a potlatch is not a potluck. A potlatch in Athabascan culture is the dinner and the party that goes along with a funeral.

In times past when they came to funerals by dog sled and it was a two or three-day trip, they didn't want to come for an hour service and then go and never be able to talk with family members and with other people in the village and so forth. So there was a social time after the funeral which came to be called a potlatch. The potlatch is sponsored by the clan of the deceased so the immediate family doesn't have to bear all the cost, and it can be right expensive.

At a potlatch there will be a number of dances and the first dance starts out to honor the deceased, to honor his memory. The family members of the deceased sit in the center of the circle and the others dance. Then they go on to one that expresses to the family we share your grief with you, we understand your loss, we mourn this loss of your loved one because he was yours but also because he was our friend. After a couple of dances along those lines, the people in the outer circle will stand back and the family members in the inner circle will do a dance to express their thanks to those who have come to share in their grief. So it's a well programmed ritual. It's becoming a lost art. Only the true elders keep up with all of it. There's a different beat to the drum for each dance and there are not a lot of youngsters who have taken up being a native drummer.

But also at a potlatch, each person who comes to share in the family's grief will be given something. You might get something as minute as a dollar bill or a soft drink or some special token to those that were involved in digging the grave. They're usually presented with a rifle, a .30/.30 rifle being the trophy of choice among the natives since it had such a background in their culture.

At several potlatches we attended we were blessed. There are what we call "potlatch blankets" that are very decorative, very beautiful. Some of them are hand done, some of them are machine done, but they're expensive and they're imported, but we were given many blankets. The missionary told us to be sure to keep some of those blankets in the plastic they came in because when we had someone within our church or within our circle of friends pass away, we could donate them to the potlatch to help the clan that was honoring the loved one that we might have had contact with.

There was an occasion in Chistochina where somehow an Alaskan state trooper who didn't understand much of Alaska and evidently none of the native culture, came to a potlatch and was going to try to arrest a man. He had gotten information that a man he wanted was a family member of the deceased. The Lord was good. We were able to get him out of that situation and explain to him that if the elders were approached, probably they would make sure that person turned himself in the next day. It was a very rude thing to take a family member from the potlatch, even though it may seem like a happy time as the dances progressed and it went into rejoicing of the person's life rather than the grieving over the loss.

A lot of the true native culture is gone. Potlatch still carries on. They have to get a special permit now from the state of Alaska to kill a moose. There are special things they do to have native dishes for a potlatch and, of course, if the moose are not in white man's season and the natives go to kill them for their ceremony then that creates problems. The state of Alaska has made special provisions and the elders of the villages can get a permit for one of their hunters to kill a moose to have moose and some of the native dishes which include moose for the loved ones in that potlatch.

I wonder what the party will be like when you're gone. Will people come to grieve because of your loss and you're no longer with them? Will they also be able, as they think on your life and as they know your testimony, to rejoice because of your life and because you're now at home with your Savior? I hope so.

Jesus Christ has created a home in heaven for each of His own. Come to Him so when the time comes they can truly have a potlatch and rejoice at your home going even as they grieve for the separation from their lives.

## CHAPTER TWENTY-TWO

## LEE

Lee had been a guide in Alaska when the Wrangell St. Elias National Park became a reality. The Bureau of Land Management and several other federal organizations greatly restricted hunting, fishing and sport activities in the park area. Virtually all of the guiding of non-resident hunters took place in that area because it was so well populated with wild life.

Lee was a very interesting character. I think he was a modern-day pirate. He learned all of their regulations. He studied them, studied them like it was law. He was an attorney and learned just how far he could do each thing. He could frustrate them because a number of times charges were made against him for illegal activities and he was able to come away from court with a not guilty because he had lived to the letter of law, not following the spirit of it at all, but to the letter of the law. It frustrated those who arrested him that didn't know the law.

The hunting regulators in the Bureau of Land Management property knew as well as he did he was getting up in age and he lived outside of Alaska. I forget exactly where he lived, but he would come back each fall for hunting season and fly a Super Cub and guide hunts in Alaska.

He became a friend just because he liked the fact I was helping the native people. He loved the native people himself and he appreciated anybody that did help them. In fact, he was a good friend of

Jack John Justin, who was a good friend of mine and actually introduced me to him.

Lee was not a religious man. I don't know if he attended church at all. We never got into that. My meetings with him were brief and public with other hunters around and all. He did on one occasion, because of what the chapel was doing for the native people, make a very large donation to the chapel out of the love for the native people and a wish for their well-being.

Lee passed away and they had a special service for him at the runway in Chistochina. The pilots flew in and we had a few thoughts and words from scripture relating to his life and his leading us. I wish I had got to know him better and known him in a more personal way, but I did enjoy the man and appreciate what he thought of the native people.

## CHAPTER TWENTY-THREE

# THE MECHANIC

There was a mechanic who lived right outside of Chistochina who tried to make a living doing equipment repair and automotive repairs. He was really struggling and didn't have much of a client base. Most people tried to do their own work and didn't pay much when they did hire somebody. He had a rough time. He didn't have any of the comforts of home; didn't have a generator. He lived a primitive lifestyle.

One Sunday morning he showed up at my door just a little bit before service time because it was cold. He walked up there because he couldn't get his vehicle running. He told me he thought he was having a heart attack and he needed to go to the hospital. He had come to me because I had a generator running most of the time and I had heaters on the car on the battery, the cooling system, and the transmission so I could virtually crank the car and move it in five minutes and have heat just a few minutes after that.

I looked at the clock and I told him there's no way I can get you to Glennallen to the hospital and get back before service time. I tried to go get him to see the health aide that lived over behind the lodge and he didn't really want to do that. I, at the time, just didn't see how I could help him and I told him that and he left. Well, I found out a while later that he indeed had had a heart attack and he had hitchhiked into Glennallen and they sent him on down to Anchorage. They had to do some kind of by-pass surgery. I don't know how extensive, but he was gone from the area and not able to work for quite some time.

Soon after he got back in the area the Lord just convicted me of how I had put the church in front of a soul that needed help. There were other people who could have led the service and I could have gone on. I just didn't think of it. The Lord convicted me to go by and speak to him and to apologize to him for having left him in his time of need and ask for his forgiveness.

He was stunned when I did. He said he had had dealings with a lot of missionaries, but he didn't know that any missionary knew how to say I'm sorry to poor people. The man was right to come to a Christian for help. I was wrong to not help him. I put the church ahead of the man. God used that to impress on me that He put divine interruptions in my life on a regular basis.

One of the other chapters in this book talks of having stopped to help a man who was in need in spite of the fact that service time was coming on and in some people's eyes I should have been in the service. Thank God He taught me that lesson first so that on the second occasion He was able to get my attention and use me at the divine interruption rather than brush someone off who may never have another chance to come to the Lord.

## CHAPTER TWENTY-FOUR

# TIME TO LOOK UP

My daddy always says when God puts you flat on your back the best thing to do is look up. It sounds like a funny thing, but it's just his way of saying it's time to look to God when you are forced to be quiet. Look to see what He has, be in step with His program and trust Him for your daily life. Sometimes we get too busy even in serving the Lord to deal with the Lord, to have a relationship with Him, and that's never God's desire. God prefers our relationship over our service.

There was a time in Alaska when I started developing some medical problems. I developed a respiratory problem that they felt like was going to go into pneumonia, so they tried to treat it but it didn't get better and I didn't want to go in the hospital. Some people would say that I'm a stubborn cuss and they're probably right.

Anyway, the doctor dealt with the situation and he told me if I would take bed rest, except for the two days that I actually had public service; the worship on Sunday at the two chapels and the Bible study on Tuesday in Slana, if I would stay in bed the rest of the time and just try to develop my strength and take the medicine he gave me he would let me stay out of the hospital. But I had to adhere to that strictly and do my best to not get tired. Well, I was already weak and getting tired was just a normal, everyday thing when I tried to get into any activity. But I much preferred being in bed at home where at least I could talk on the telephone, and sometimes I did counseling by telephone. In my own bed I could do some reading and some studying and preparing.

The Chistochina Chapel at that time gave me a Dremel tool so I could work at making some knife handles, which had been a hobby of mine prior to going to Alaska, because they thought I wouldn't do well being idle. They were right. They knew me pretty well.

One of the things I did while I was resting, I took an old Bible that had been around for a long time (like most preachers I have a number of Bibles in various translations, and this was just a good old King James that I had grown up with) and I read through it cover to cover. I started in Genesis all the way through the Revelation. I underlined each verse that I came upon that I realized I had memorized in times past.

After I had finished reading it I came back around and I tried to figure out where I learned the verses. I tried to put them in some perspective. Was there a lesson that I learned in Sunday school? Was it someone who had taught me? I came upon 127 verses that my grandmother Pearce taught me.

That's rather notable when you realize that I moved away from her on my 9th birthday and never lived near her again except for a very brief period after I got out of the Army when I was married.

So she was right active in teaching me to love God's word at that time. As my parents began a deeper walk with the Savior they taught me a lot. They taught me to love God, to love His word.

As things developed, they found out that I had a gallstone. I found out the way my sister said they would have found out in the mountains of Guatemala when they weren't sure if it was a heart attack or a gallbladder. What they do is give a person an apple to eat and something in the apple triggers a secretion from the gallbladder and if there's a problem in the gallbladder it becomes real apparent. It's very painful, but at least you know it's the gallbladder and not the heart.

Well, I wasn't trying to find out if I had a gallbladder problem. I was hungry and we didn't get a lot of fruit, but for some reason there was a fresh apple somebody had brought out of Glennallen and it was on the counter. I ate that apple and just a very brief time later I was in mortal pain. I knew I was having a heart attack. I would have been just as happy to die. It hurt too much to keep going.

A neighbor, Bev, took me into Glennallen because it was late at night and my wife wasn't able to drive me at that particular time. I remember going by the airport at Gakona on the Richardson Highway she started laughing but I couldn't understand what it was; it was just sort of detached.

Later on, after I had been in the hospital and they had given me a lot of morphine to ease the pain and sent me on into Anchorage where they removed my gallbladder, I asked her what was so funny that she would laugh when I was hurting as bad as I was. She said that I must have become delirious because just about the time we passed the airport somehow I knocked my hat off and I was stomping it into the floorboard screaming I was having a baby. She did find that quite humorous and I did too later, but I was so out of it I didn't know it at the time.

While I was in Anchorage having the surgery, which I had at the Catholic hospital where they did a beautiful job taking care of me, the priest came by and asked me if he could pray with me and he really treated me like royalty. A family, a lady and several of her kids, hitchhiked about 600 miles roundtrip to come to the hospital to see that I was all right and tell me they were praying for me. That was a very humbling experience to see that God had laid me on their hearts to that extent. They were a blessing to me at that time.

When I got back out it was a while before I gained my strength. I was getting cabin fever. I was tired of being in the house. My wife had gone off somewhere and I was home alone and just couldn't stand being in that little trailer any longer, so I put my parka on and eased on over to the neighbors. A lot of people would get confused because the neighbor's house was on the same driveway as the chapel, but it was before the chapel. The actual parsonage where I lived was off to the side. If you were coming down the driveway and weren't familiar, you wouldn't even see that until you got right down to the chapel.

Well, a native, who was highly intoxicated, had wandered in knowing that the chapel was down there and he was coming to find the preacher to ask him to give him a ride back to Gakona. It was about 27 or 28 miles away. He knocked on the door to the neighbor's house. When she opened the door he said, "You've got to give me a ride to Gakona." She spoke right out: "I don't have to give you a ride anywhere." He said, "I put money in the plate at Gakona and it's all the same mission, you-all need to give me a ride. She said, "No, no. I can't give you a ride."

He looked at me and I really shouldn't have been out of bed yet, I was extremely weak and tired. He said, "You give me a ride." She said, "He can't give you a ride. He just had surgery and he's sick." She said, "This isn't the preacher's house. He said, "Well, where's the preacher's house?" She said, "It's over there behind the chapel but he's not there now and he won't be back there for a while, he's sick." The man looked at her and said, "This is an unhealthy neighborhood." He walked on out. I'm sure he found a way home because we never saw him on the road after that.

The Lord worked a lot in that. The downtime, the quiet time was precious because I spent more time with Him, more time in His word. I came back to full strength and was able to work again, but God had also taught me that it was time to pace myself, that I couldn't do it all. I needed to prioritize and do item one and item two and whatever I got down to at the end of the day, if I hadn't finished that particular task, I needed to either let it go or reprioritize it into tomorrow's schedule. I couldn't run myself the way I had.

God gave me time to be with Him and I thank Him for it. Time in His Word is precious. Time with His people is precious. Don't waste time. Spend a little time with Him every day. He loves you and you'll grow to love Him more as you spend time with Him and develop a relationship and find out who He really is.

## CHAPTER TWENTY-FIVE

## THE FIGHTER

I had a friend who ran a school bus route, covered over 100 miles every day picking up kids and taking them down to Glenallen to the high school. He told me a story about how he had hired different drivers and they all had problems with these two boys that wanted to fight. One was a white boy and one was a native. And no matter what you did with them, sooner or later sometime during the day they'd get in a fight.

He couldn't get anybody else to take that route, so he took it himself. Sure enough he picked them up the first day, got up the road a little ways and they started fighting. He pulled the school bus over to the side of the road and he jumped out, grabbed the two of them, and threw them off the bus. He took them out behind the school bus and told them if you want to fight, fight. Every time one of them slowed down, he'd boot him in the butt a little bit and get them back and say, come on, you've got to fight, fight, and fight. And they kept fighting until they were just worn out, couldn't even stand up. And then he was prodding them both, come on, you want to fight, let's fight, come on fight. Of course all the other kids on the school bus were watching it.

The interesting thing is the two guys got to be the best of friends later on as they grew up. I don't know that they never got in another fight, but they never got into another one that created that many problems. The school bus driver showed a lot of wisdom in handling people.

I think it's sort of like God. A lot of times God would show us what He wants us to do, give us directions for our lives and somehow we just don't want to do it and we'll go our own way. God will say, okay, you can go that way and because of my grace you're saved. You're going to heaven because you have a relationship with me. I won't make you do what I want; I'll let you go your own way.

Sooner or later circumstances and things will just fade away. Mark Lowry sings the song "*I Worship at the Shrine of Plenty*" and he talks about all the things of the world, gold and silver, turning to rust. That's true in the Christian life, for the things we seek never give us the satisfaction that God gives us when we are walking in His way for our lives. Sooner or later, because we've had our own way and we've worn out our own way, we'll come back to walk with Him. I trust you're walking with God now. If you're walking away from Him, if you're fighting God, He'll let you win for now, but He loves you and wants you back walking with Him in your daily life. He has blessings that go on for eternity, His protection, His care, His guidance, His presence.

A preacher preaches about the exchanged life quite often. He wants us to give up our old life and let Him live His life through us for His honor and glory and our wellbeing. The safest place in the world is dead in the middle of God's will.

# CHAPTER TWENTY-SIX

## THE MISSIONARY AND THE MOUSE

This is one that was related to me by friends who were missionaries in Alaska. Someone in their village had tried to give their little daughter a kitten. The mother did not want a kitten or a cat or anything to do with them. It created a little family controversy. After dinner that evening the little girl brought it up again. Her momma said there's nothing in the world I hate more than cats. Naturally the little girl said, but this is a kitten. Her momma said it'll grow up to be a cat. Daddy said honey, to the little girl, why don't you just ask Jesus about that tonight. Just do what He says and we'll not upset the whole family.

So sure enough come bedtime the little girl kneeled down by her bed. After her usual request of blessings to various family members and friends and all she said, "And Jesus, please let me have a kitten." The daddy was listening to the prayer that night and he sort of snickered. He didn't see how that was going to work out.

He went and crawled in bed with his wife and turned out the light and almost immediately something fell out of the rafters of their cabin and hit momma right between the eyes and scurried off. They got the light on in time to see a mouse running across the floor. Sure enough momma decided there was one thing that she hated worse than cats and that was mice.

The little girl got her kitten. She had it until a ripe old age and it had passed away by the time I had heard the story. God answers prayers, not always the way we ask, not always the way we want, but he answers prayers. Somebody said He answers it yes, no, or wait a while. I think there's a fourth one. Butch Morrison has preached on that. Yes, I'll do what you ask, that will be it; no, you need to change your mind because that's not my program. It's one of the things God says all too often. James says we ask and we have not because we ask amiss. Wait, Grandma Pearce says it's the weight that broke the wagon. Everybody's heard that. Nobody likes to wait, but sometimes they have to. The fourth is My grace is sufficient for thee.

The Apostle Paul asked three times for his thorn in the flesh to be removed and wrote his testimony, my grace is sufficient is what God had said. And so he went on to live his life, trusting God to carry him through.

Are you praying? Are you seeing answers? Are you deciphering what God's answer to your prayer is?

The story is told about a little boy who had a withered hand and he prayed, God, make my one hand like the other. And sure enough the next morning he got up and his other hand was withered too. It's a terrible joke, but it's a reality. So often we pray in such a way that God would hardly recognize what the answer should be in our minds. So it's hard to say yes, no, or maybe or My grace is sufficient because we haven't defined what our prayers are. It's just God bless this and God bless that and go on down the road.

God listens to our prayers and answers according to His will. Walk with Him and He'll touch your heart, He'll lead you in what to pray for and then He'll give you His answer. God bless you as you pray.

## CHAPTER TWENTY-SEVEN

# BIG JOHN

I met a lady in Slana who was married to a man who was adamant about not being involved in the church and being happy with God and he faced a lot of problems in his life and that was understandable. He had gone to Anchorage for eye surgery. The total time I'd been in Slana he had never come around to meet me. He didn't want me to preach so he just stayed away.

One Sunday afternoon she stopped me after service and said, "My husband is in Anchorage; he's had eye surgery on one eye and we don't have a telephone, don't have any communications, don't know when he's coming home, don't know if they're going to operate on the other eye or what they're going to do, but I know you're going to Anchorage this week, would you stop and see him." She gave me an address and gave me his name and told me that he probably wouldn't be real happy with the preacher, but she needed information and if I could help please try and pray for him. She truly loved this man.

I told her I would. Part of being God's servant is being a messenger, and sometimes the message you deliver is something besides Bible study, it's helping people get what they need to get on with their lives.

So I went on into Anchorage. Actually, what I was doing was taking Mom and Dad back to fly back out to Wisconsin. Dad was waiting in the truck. Momma had gone to do some shopping. Dad said,

"I'll just stay here and pray for you. With him, knowing the situation, we don't want to crowd him and upset him. I'll be praying and you do whatever the Lord leads."

So I went and knocked on the door and this great big fellow answered the door. He wasn't particularly happy at the time. I told him that I was a friend of his wife's from Slana and real quick he said, "You're the preacher." I said, "Yes, yes, that's true. I was just coming to see how you're doing. Any message I can carry to your wife or whatever to let her know what's going on, she's concerned?"

He said, "You can come in but I don't want you preaching at me." I said, "Well, I'll respect that, sir. I just wanted to know how you're doing." And he went on and told me life had been rough for him. He had been to Viet Nam and was the only one to survive an attack on a vehicle he was in that left him disabled. He went back to Seattle and then had problems there. Someone who had been in partnership with him in a business had messed him up. They ran off with the money and left him with the bills. I don't remember all the details, but it was a struggle.

He had come to Alaska and hadn't been able to get going doing anything. He had eye problems and they told him they'd operate on the one eye and see what happened and then they would determine what they were going to do after that. They operated and the eye wasn't healing real well. He had just come away from an appointment where they had told him that he lived in Slana and people in Slana don't work and they weren't going to give him a free eye operation on the other eye. He was just going to have to make do the best he could. They hadn't given him his final release yet, so he couldn't head back for Homestead Village.

We finished our visit and it was right at the end that I asked him what his plans were. He said, well, he had one more appointment Monday and he didn't know what was going to happen after that. He was going to have to hitchhike back. He didn't have a vehicle and nobody would give him a ride. He had already been told there would be no operation on the other eye, so he probably wasn't going to be too far behind me when I headed up the road.
So I asked him if I could pray with him, and he, probably just out of respect because I listened to his story, said okay. He was reluctant, but he allowed me to pray. I just asked God to work in this man's life and for Him to undertake for him and provide what was necessary, even the operation on the second eye and healing of the first eye if that was in His will; that He would give grace to this man and allow him to have a life worthwhile where he'd be able to support his family.

Well, I packed up and left. I dropped Mom and Dad off at the airport and went on back. I reported to the lady when we had the Bible study that week what had happened and told her his extended plans were that sometime early in the week after he was clear of that last appointment and had his temporary apartment all cleaned up he would be hitchhiking up the road. He'd send her a clatter on the mission radio station, which was just a public announcement, to say hey this is John, and he'd list his wife by name and tell her he was starting home such-a -such a day. She'd have to figure how long it would take him to hitchhike close to 300 miles.

We didn't hear anything. There wasn't any news at all. No message on the Clatters. They were broadcast twice a day and everybody would listen to them because that was probably the source of most gossip in the valley, but also the only communication. It was just one-way communication for the people out in the bush who didn't have telephones.

Well, life dragged on and that week we didn't hear anything. The next Sunday we were in service and I was sitting there in the front row. We had a lady who led the singing and often led the prayer time. We were singing *How Great Thou Art*. The door opened and closed. People came and went in the Homestead community right regular and you didn't embarrass anybody by turning to look to see who came in or who left or whatever.

On the next verse I heard that bass voice singing *How Great Thou Art* and I knew big John had gotten back and he had come to church. He hadn't gone home yet. Service had started before he got home. So, of course, his wife was real excited when she heard him singing it. He hadn't been to church in many years.

It came time for our prayer and praise time and he stood up and he said, "I'm just thankful we've got a preacher that prays." He sat down and that's all he said. Of course, we didn't know what had happened yet. At the close of the service he snuck out. He didn't stay around and talk to everybody.

I felt like I needed to make contact so I went on up to the house and spoke with him. He told me what had happened there. He went in on that Monday appointment to see his counselor, who had already told him virtually that he wasn't going to get another eye operation because he wasn't worth it, and he got in there and went to report to his counselor and his counselor was gone. They said he quit, he left. You're going to have to speak with a new counselor.

So he went in to speak with the new counselor and the counselor said, well, bring me up to speed, tell me what's going on because I'm just starting the day on this other man's cases and I don't know a whole lot about it. I've got these little bits of records here so help me out. John told him. He said he was told there wasn't going to be another eye operation. They've got to look at this eye and he thought he could release me, so how about just finish up and let me go on home.

The counselor asked him, "Well, why are they not going to operate on your other eye when this first eye is not doing real well?" He said, "We're not going to send you back to the bush to just be blind. John said, "Well, they told me there's not going to be another eye operation, so I don't know. The man turned around, looked at a phone directory, and dialed a number and spoke to someone. He looked up at John and he said, "Sir, can you be prepared for surgery at 8 o'clock tomorrow morning on your other eye?" John was elated and said he certainly would be.

The next morning they did that surgery. As time went on the other eye got better and he was able to see pretty well with both eyes.

He got back to the village and he didn't have a lot to say, he still kept to himself. The next week he came to church. During praise time he stood up and said, "I thank God. For the first time in years I've seen the colors in the leaves change. I can see." He then sat down. The Lord was good and the Lord was working in his life.

The next week John had decided it was time to let people know he had a relationship with God. He went around to every Christian in the village, asked their forgiveness. He said, "I am a Christian. I'm a brother in Christ. I've been mad at God and I've taken it out on every Christian that I could and I'm sorry that I've hurt you and ask forgiveness."

He went to a fellow who always gave him a ride to the post office, which is a couple miles down the road, and he told that fellow the same thing. The guy was a real nice fellow who helped everybody out. John assumed he was a Christian. He told the guy that he got right with God and that he was sorry; that he didn't mean to offend him and asked him to forgive him. The man said, "You've gone religious nuts. I'm not a Christian, leave me alone, and get out of here." So he ran him off.

On the next mail day he didn't stop by and pick John up to give him a ride to the post office. So John set out and walked, I guess about four miles one way, and got his mail and walked home. The next week there was a lot of water. It was raining, and I don't remember whether it was fall and the rains were coming before the snow or whether it was spring and thawing, but anyway there was a lot of water in the village.  John had set out walking to the post office and this neighbor who usually picked him up saw him, waited until he got right up alongside this great big mud puddle and he roared through in his four-by-four and splashed him, about half drowned him, and kept on going.  John just kept walking.

He got up the road a little ways and there was the man in his four-by-four with a flat tire.  The man had some medical problems of his own and he wasn't really able to break loose the nuts to change the tire. John was a big, strong man.  John very graciously said I'll be glad to help you change that tire.  The man just backed up and let John jack the car up, get the lug nuts loose and get the wheel off and get the spare on it.  He handed the man the jack handle back and he started to walk down the road.  The man looked at him and said, "If you promise not to preach this religious stuff I'll give you a ride to the post office."  John got in, rode to the post office.

That man got a sermon that day.  God tells us to love our enemies.  This man truly had done everything to be an enemy to John and John showed love, showed God's love.  He was willing to stop and help him, then go down the road walking if that's what it took.

I don't know if the man ever came to know the Lord.  John was a testimony to Slana Village of God's grace.  He's still a good friend.  I hear from them every Christmas.  They are wonderful people.  God changes hearts and God is willing to change yours. God's willing to give you love for that enemy, that ex, whatever.  God's willing to touch your heart and give you love for him.  Give up your prejudice, give up your hatred, let God come into your heart and fill you with His love so it can spill out so you can love others.

## CHAPTER TWENTY-EIGHT

# OLE

A lot of happy wanderers go through Alaska. Some people feel the wander lust and they hitchhike through just to see Alaska the way the natives do. Others come looking for a place to settle down out of sight of the government so they can homestead or maybe buy a place if they ever get money and find work. But a lot of interesting characters flow through the small villages of Alaska.

I was over at the Chistochina Lodge one day and there was a tall, muscular, military-looking man. He spoke very little English. I tried to greet him to see how he was doing and to be sociable but he didn't communicate very well. I went on about my business.

A few days later I was at the lodge, where I ended up almost every day. That was where we bought fuel and bread and the little things we needed. It was the only source of a Pepsi or Dr. Pepper in town. We kept up friendships and relationships there and it was where we got messages from the villagers.

Anyway, as I was there again this same fellow was there. He was doing some chores around the lodge, obviously trading out for something to eat. I had spoken with Terry, who ran the lodge, asked her who he was and what the deal was. She said, "Well, he's Ole." He had come in through Canada, walked across the border and gotten stopped by the Alaska State Troopers. They found out that he wasn't an

American citizen and he had to go through a hearing. They would notify him of the hearing and the only address he had for communication was the Chistochina lodge because that's where he was stopped.

They were willing to try to help him there. They were very hospitable people and helped a lot of folks and they were willing to help him. There was a great communication problem though. I found out that he was of Norwegian decent but I didn't know exactly why he came or where he came from. The communication just wasn't that good and I always felt like maybe he hadn't told us everything, maybe he didn't want to communicate real well.

One thing led to another and they needed a place for him to stay while he was waiting for his hearing, which was probably going to be about three to four weeks. There was an old eight-foot wide mobile home right behind the chapel that had been used for a Sunday school room at one time. I don't know if it had ever been a residence. It was leveled, but it had just kerosene lamps and a little oil heater. There was no sign of it ever having been set up to live in or if it had been they just used an outhouse. So I went over and looked at that and decided we could clean it out and make room for him just to help this stranger in need.

So I went and spoke with Chuck Hermans, my neighbor who was the treasurer of the chapel, and asked him about it. He said that would be fine, anything we could do to help someone and maybe be a witness to show him God's love, so I went over. Terry was the best one at communicating with him and I explained to her what the options were. It was a place fit for just one person. It had a little tiny cot and it had fuel oil, enough to last for maybe a month. If he wanted to stay there until he had his hearing he was welcome, but it would be just for him. He was very kind, very happy to be able to do that. I thought Terry had communicated with him right well.

We got the heater going that day while he was working his chores at the lodge. By the time he finished up that evening and went over it was warm and he had a cozy little place. He stayed there about three days and then he just disappeared. Well, I had been in law enforcement 15 years by that time and I was used to seeing people come and when they'd get too familiar or somebody might find out who they really were or where they were from or what they were up to they would go on down the road.

I had seen it for a year or two in Alaska by then too, so it didn't surprise me. I just thought, well, we'd done our part and that didn't work out, we didn't communicate well. I had hoped that maybe he got the message God loved him, but we couldn't be sure because of the communication gap.

But he was gone about three days. I was getting ready to go do my calling, which I always did in the afternoon, and I stepped outside and cranked the car, let it warm up a bit and heard somebody in the snow. I looked out and there was Ole coming up the driveway going across behind the chapel to the little trailer.

Well, I knew it was going to be cold because it had been three days since the old heater had been on. We turned it off since he wasn't around and he hadn't left anything there so we didn't know that he was coming back and he hadn't communicated to anybody. But very quickly I noticed there was somebody behind him a little smaller. I didn't recognize him. He was all wrapped up in a parka and hunched over into the cold. I couldn't tell if it was a man or a woman.

Well, I waited a few minutes until he'd had time to light his heater and decided I'd go over and find out who his new friend was and what was going on and see if he had heard anything about his hearing. Well, I got over there and found that he had gone to Canada and come back across the border. He had picked up a French-speaking lady and brought her back and was going to live there with her. Well, we didn't do a whole lot better with the French than we did with the Norwegian.

I went over to Chuck, who was right next door, and said, "Chuck, you know we've got a problem and I need help. I don't know what the deal is and we can't seem to communicate." Chuck said, "Well, let's get them into your place where it's warm and we can talk and maybe we'll manage to communicate somehow and get the message across.

So I went and knocked on the door again and told them that they needed to come to my house, we needed to talk. They came over. I was standing there in front of them speaking and Chuck was behind me. Now, keep in mind Chuck's about six-foot three and he's an old Navy man, he has a commanding presence. Throw on a wool shirt and a parka and a coonskin cap and he's a right tough looking individual. He was right behind me and I was doing my best to communicate and just wasn't getting through. Then all of a sudden Ole just sort of motioned okay and shrugged his shoulders and pointed to her that she would have to leave.

Before I had a chance to get too elated with my mastery of communication I noticed in the mirror on the wall Chuck behind me, standing there shaking his head in that coonskin cap that he had. He looked so big and impressive, almost like Daniel Boone or Davy Crocket. He had communicated with a shake of the head far better than I was able to do with all of my struggling words. Soon after that Ole disappeared and I never saw him in Chistochina again. I don't know if he ended up getting his hearing and became a citizen or got deported or what.

We just tried being a Good Samaritan and somehow the situation got out of hand. God is good. We were able to help some people even though they may never have understood we were able to help them because God loved them. God loved them anyway. I hope that somehow down the road that Ole and his friend managed to find someone who could communicate the love of Jesus Christ to them.

# CHAPTER TWENTY-NINE

## PERSPECTIVE

When we went to Chistochina, naturally a number of folks who had been there before related different things to try to help us fit in and understand what the village was and who the villagers were, just to help us in our orientation. One missionary told the story about coming to Alaska from another mission field. He was completing his work for his doctorate, if I recall correctly, and was assigned to Chistochina. Several people from the village had come to help him move in. He had never lived in the Alaskan bush and he'd never lived with the Alaskan people before.

When they finished getting things off the truck and were pausing for a break, he sat down with one of the village elders who asked him something about where he'd come from and, in his mind, his qualifications. The missionary was very proud of where he had come from and his qualifications and he listed them. He told them he had a bachelor's degree from such and such a college and he had a master's from another university and another master's degree from another university in a different field of study. He was presently getting ready to complete his work for his Doctorate of Divinity.

The village elder looked at him and asked him quietly, can you skin a moose? So often our perspectives are not exactly what God's perspectives are, yet we want to decide who or what fits into God's program. God in His grace includes all who will come to Him. What are the qualifications? Just a contrite heart, to admit you're a sinner. You need to ask Him to forgive your sins and to come into your life. By His mercy, He will forgive your sins.

Do you have to be a doctor of divinity to be qualified to serve Him? No. Do you have to know how to skin a moose to serve Him? No. You have to be available for whatever He calls you to do. God wants you to use every talent you have.

Another chapter in this book talks about nothing wasted, and really God wastes nothing. If it's available to Him, He'll use it for His honor and glory and for your good and the good of the folks around you; for the good of His church, the body of believers, and the good of the world that hasn't even come to the Savior yet because He loves all men.
God bless you. Keep things in perspective.

## CHAPTER THIRTY

# CHISTOCHINA GOLD

Everybody associates Alaska with gold and they think of the prospectors and the sourdoughs and the guys who struck it rich and hit the mother lode. It just seems to fit so well with the Alaskan motif. There is a lot of gold panning still done in small independent mines. Some just stake out a claim and they have to take a certain amount of gold out of it every year to maintain that claim. I'm not familiar with all those regulations.

Chisto was just sort of a non-place, a wide spot on the road on the Tok cutoff. It's about 50 miles from Glennallen and about 90 miles from Tok on the Glennallen Highway. You turned off at Gakona Village and went on up through. None of the tour buses and not many of the tourists stopped at Chistochina Lodge.

Chistochina had a beautiful lodge. It was an old lodge that burned to the ground and has since been rebuilt. Its trademark was a bear, a big concrete statue of a bear, up over the door on the roof. The bear was down on all fours like he was feeding somewhere with his neck stretched out. It was a beautiful statue. I don't know the history of it, who made it or why it ended up there.

One winter night we were sitting there, nobody around, sitting around the wood stove brain storming. Some of the folks who ran the lodge were involved in it, and me. The conversation came up about what could we do that might trigger the tour buses to stop here, that might draw tourists' attention; so that we'd get a little bit of this money that's coming into the valley but doesn't seem to stop here.

Through our brainstorming we came up with the idea of getting the little cans like they can salmon in, about a half-pound, and throwing some of the black sand in there where they find gold so often and then putting a few flakes of gold in each can. We would seal them up, just like they were sealed for salmon to keep it fresh.

The idea was to put a label on it that said Chistochina Gold. I've still got the first can because they presented it to me since I was part of the brainstorming session. They would sell the can and a vial to put the gold flakes in. They would then take you outside to a little water trough and you'd open the can, empty it into the pan and they would show you how to pan for the gold and how to identify it. They would show you how to get it out of the can and put it in the little vial to take home your flakes. And included in the price of the can and the vial and the instruction was also a Polaroid picture of you panning for gold.

The idea went over real big, and the next year there was a lot of traffic in the Chistochina lodge. When you get a tour bus of 45or 50 people, it's going to take them all a while to go through and pan for their gold. Most of them would buy five or six cans and take some home. They would just pan one and learn how to do it and then take one home to each of the kids or grandma or whoever. They bought the little gold pans so they could show the people how to pan it with a real gold pan.

Obviously, when people are waiting around they've got to do something else, so the tourist trade picked up, the restaurant business picked up. Chisto burgers sold like hotcakes.

The Chisto burger was a great thing. It was a hamburger patty and a chicken patty on the same bun. It doesn't sound real good, but it went together so well. It had lettuce and tomato when they were in season and they could get them. It was a delicious sandwich. There were great people and there was great fellowship around the tables there at the Chistochina Lodge.

A lot of people struck gold at the Chistochina Lodge. Of course, like every other great idea, people copied it. By the next year every lodge along the Alaskan highway or any of the roads in the interior of Alaska had a trough with their own cans of gold to sell. It was a great idea. There were a lot of stories that came out, and a lot of books about prospecting for gold were sold at the lodge. It was always intriguing to people when you actually see a gold operation to read the history of some others.

Not far from Chistochina Lodge the greatest gold producing mine in Alaska worked up at the end of Nebesna Road for many years. It has since closed down, if my information is correct. People came to Alaska looking for gold; some of them found God. Some of them just suffered and became sourdoughs. The Alaskan definition of a sourdough is a guy soured in Alaska and not enough dough to get out.

Anyway, I hope you didn't go looking for gold and miss it. I hope you did go looking for God and found Him because He's available to you. He loves you. He wants to give you the good times, not just gold, but Himself to walk with through this life and into eternity. God bless you all.

## CHAPTER THIRTY-ONE

# BEAR?

One of the first missionaries in Chistochina was pretty much loved in the valley. In fact, he stayed on. He'd left the mission for whatever reason and went to work at the Copper Valley power company down in Glennallen. Glennallen had a power station and power generator. They clicked on the lights without a generator making a noise in the backyard and it worked. We didn't have that privilege out in Chistochina.

Anyway, old Joe was much loved by the people up there and was quite a joker. He loved to tease and teased people in good natured ways. I heard a lot of times when they'd talk about Joe they'd say well, when you see him ask him if he knows the difference between a bear and a St. Bernard. Nobody would ever tell me what the story was about, but they'd always say ask him about the bear and the St. Bernard.

I was a flight instructor and one day Joe called me and said, "Al, I need a biannual flight review. I've got to ride with a flight instructor in my little old Champ, I wonder if you'll help me out on that, get me certified for another two years so I can go ahead and fly around Alaska." I said, "Sure, I'd be glad to. Meet me up at the airstrip in Chistochina." He said, "What's it going to cost?" I said, "Well, you're going to have to buy me a Chisto burger at the lodge, sit and keep me company while I eat it, and you're going to have to tell me why everybody asks you

'What is the difference between a St. Bernard and a bear?'." He said, "Well, I'll do that."

A few days later we met at the airstrip and did a nice flight review. He's an excellent pilot. He had a nice little Champ. I think it was a 7ECA, if I'm not mistaken, 100 horsepower with an electrical system, and tundra tires on it. It was a true small Alaskan plane.

We finished up the flight review and went in and ordered our Chisto burgers and sat and enjoyed them. We kicked back and I got my Dr. Pepper ready. I'm ready just to relax and enjoy. I was waiting for the story. He told me about some folks who had lived right next to the chapel in the house that Chuck and Bev Hermans had bought and lived in while I was there. I'm not even sure whether it was the same cabin, just the same location.

Anyway, they got to be good friends and things were going along well. It was his first year in Chistochina, and I guess the first year in the bush in Alaska. He got a caribou and stored it under a truck cover, hard shell top cover, and figured it was okay because of the cold weather. They would sort of keep it and slice off bits and pieces like the rest of the Alaskans did. He got up the next morning and a bear had gone and torn up his camper and had carted off all of his caribou and eaten it.

Well, this upset Joe. He was not too hospitable to the bear. He had his winter's meat and now all of a sudden he's used his tag, he can't go get another one, and doesn't have anything to eat for the winter. Well, he decided he was going to get that bear. Sure enough the next night or so the bear came back and dumped over his garbage can and spilled that all over the yard. He said, "Well, that's going to do it." He put something real tasty and smelly in the garbage can, sat out on the porch, a 30/30 laid across his lap. It got dark and it got cold and he sort of scrunched down and went to sleep.

He woke up hearing this terrible noise and he knew that bear had gotten in his garbage can again. He raised up that 30/30 and fired one shot. He killed that thing dead as a hammer right there. He went out there to look at it. He had killed the neighbor's St. Bernard dog.

I don't know how that did for the relationship at the time. They evidently got over it because they all teased him about it. Nobody would ever tell the outsiders the story, Joe had to tell them himself.

## CHAPTER THIRTY-TWO

# HITCHHIKER

A lot of people in Alaska didn't have transportation, didn't have a lot of money, and they got down the road by hitchhiking. They often hitch hiked long distances and sometimes almost as whole families. There would be three or four people traveling together. I always felt like the Lord called me to the people of Alaska, not just the ones I was going to see, but the ones I saw on the way. I had a hard time passing up a hitchhiker because here I was collecting mileage from a mission and they're paying to run my car so I could drive to tell people about Jesus. I couldn't just drive past people on the road. It didn't make sense.

Anyway, as a regular thing I picked up hitchhikers. I'd been a cop for 15 years before I went to Alaska and I felt like the Lord was going to take care of me, and He probably prepared me for most emergencies that I would handle. When I was out in the bush I always carried a .44 Magnum in the summertime when the bears were moving. I carried a .22, a .22 Smith and Wesson camp gun in the wintertime to shoot a rabbit and take it to the elders as I went to visit them. You know, I usually had my protection, but it was usually in the trunk of the car if I wasn't out in the bush itself. I did carry a buck knife between the seats, the split front seat of that '78 Mercury Cougar.

A lot of times I just felt it was good to have it there. I never had to use it for anything but the traditional chores. If you were out in the bush, and were a long ways from a toolbox, you always wanted a good knife and Leatherman and a few other handy things because you were dealing with mechanical things all the time.

Anyway, I was coming out of Glennallen one night in late summertime. The sun was still bright at 10:30 or 11 o'clock at night. I had been to the hospital to do a visit. As I was coming up to the Dairy Queen there was a guy hitchhiking. I pulled over and said, "Hop in, which way are you heading?" He said he was heading for Tok. "I'm going to North Way and then on down through Canada going back to the lower 48."

So I went ahead and started up the road and we started talking and by the time I got to my driveway 50 miles away – he'd stopped for a break once or twice – he was telling me how the FBI hypnotized him and used him to rape women and get information from them, even killed a man, and used him as a plant to break up a lot of things. It seemed like maybe there were some problems there. I found out his profession and he was a cook. I didn't know the FBI used a bunch of cooks for that kind of stuff.

I decided when I got to my driveway if I stopped and let him out there he was going to be hanging in the neighborhood. I just felt better if he went on down the road. There was an old retired Alaskan state trooper who ran a store up in Slana out on the highway, just down the road from Duffy's Tavern. I thought, if this was a problem child that was hanging around the neighborhood that would be a good place for him to hang around because I knew the old trooper still had contacts; he'd get things checked out.

Anyway, I took him on up and turned on Nebesna Road and told him he could go on the road from there going to Tok. He took off, hoofed it up the road. I think he was familiar with Duffy's Tavern because he headed right up there. I stopped to see Jim Hummell, the park ranger. Jim had basically a small police station right there and he had teletype access. We tried to check and see if this guy was missing from a mental hospital or something. We couldn't account for him.

I went on home and went to bed. It's now about 2:30 or 3 o'clock in the morning. It wasn't too long before Ernie Charlie was knocking on the door. Ernie was the son of Jerry Charlie, the chief of the village. He'd won a Citabria airplane in a raffle and he was familiar but he hadn't had any flying lessons because there weren't any flying instructors around. He could fly the thing, but he wanted to get his license. So being the only flight instructor I would give him lessons now and again and Ernie and I became friends.

Ernie's problem that day was he was working on the road crew on the highway department and the bulldozer broke down and they needed a part that you could get at Tok and they needed it quick. Well, the foreman of the crew knew that Ernie didn't have a pilot's license so he couldn't authorize him to go fly and pick up something for the company, but he said if Ernie could get a licensed pilot or a flight instructor to go with him to pick up the part he'd pay the expenses for the trip.

Ernie was always ready to fly any chance he got and I was too. We got in the old Citabria there in Chistochina, flew up to Tok. We were walking from the airport across the road to the parts distributor for the needed equipment and guess who I ran into? Yes, my old hitchhiker. I told Ernie if that fellow acts like he knows me, I want you to act like the meanest, craziest native you've ever been in your life and run that boy off. Ernie just laughed and said, "There's a story I know".

Anyway, we left him there. He didn't recognize me and didn't say anything. We picked up the parts and went on home. About three days later I stopped in at Duffy's Tavern. It was sort of a point of call for most everybody from Slana or the highway where everybody met. It was another lodge. They called it Duffy's, but it was just another lodge.

I went in there and drank a Mountain Dew and talked to some people. I got back in the car and started back to Chistochina. Guess who was there? Yep, there's my old hitchhiker. I decided it was just better to go home this time, so I just went on home. I never saw the hitchhiker again. I don't know if he was a FBI plant for anything. I figure he was about as crazy as a bed bug and he was just another interesting character. I never did get a name from him. He talked too much to ever give me his name.

The wonderful thing is God knows his name and Jesus loves him. I don't know what mental problems he had. I don't know what spiritual problems he had, but I know God was able to fix them. I hope that sometime the fellow was quiet enough to listen to God, whether it was through somebody picking him up on the road or whatever. He's known to God.

## CHAPTER THIRTY-THREE

# MR. BELT

One of the things that I was able to do at the Slana church: several of the people wanted a Bible study but it wasn't practical to keep the church open an extra day of the week so we'd have it in Wanda and Don Craig's home in a cabin in back of Slana. In wet season when it was melting or raining you pretty much had to walk. Whenever it was frozen you could drive back there. We had a good time. A lot of times there would be a dozen people sitting in there. I met Don Craig there and he's now gone to be with the Lord. He was a precious fellow.

He had hurt his back in Washington and had enough disability he figured that he could survive on his disability pay in Alaska by homesteading and growing vegetables, in a nice greenhouse which he set up. He knew agriculture and knew how to make things work. He wasn't able to do heavy work because of his back injury. People told me that he didn't like preachers, he didn't like some preachers.
I went to meet him. His wife was very active in the Slana church and kept the church going. Wanda was the backbone of the church, along with two other ladies, and also the nearest thing to a nurse they had in Slana. So a lot of things happened in and around their house. It was a real center of activity. It was almost a community house; although it was just a family dwelling.

I went in to see Don and meet him. He was weeding his garden. He couldn't bend over because of his back injury, but what he would do was sit on the ground and pull the weeds and then he'd slide along a little bit and pull some more weeds. Well, if you're going to meet a man you've got to meet him where he is, so I sat down on the other side of the row of whatever it was. I don't remember what he was growing in that particular plot, but I started weeding and talking. By the time we got to the end of that first row together we were friends. He took to me; he was very kind to me.

When we got to the end of the row he sat there a minute and he said, "Preacher, I'd like to go to a Bible study but the pews at church I just can't sit in." He said he had a hard time with crowds. He said, "If I could sit by my own stove and I'd feed the fire and get out and go to the outhouse when I need to and sort of just relax and be me, I'd sure love to have a Bible study in my house." Well, that's what I'd come to ask him about. And I had a feeling Wanda sort of forewarned him because she didn't want him to be blindsided in the thing.

But anyway, we started Bible study on Tuesday afternoons. We'd start around 2 o'clock. I didn't have to wear my black jeans for that because it was just a Bible study, so I'd go in blue jeans. I always ended up doing extra things along the way. We'd sit there and there'd be anywhere from a half a dozen up to one particular occasion when there were 27. This is in a two-bedroom log cabin with the living room that was big enough for 27 people, but there was a bunch of people sitting on the floor. You would have to be careful not to bump the stove because everybody is real close and you're not far from the stove.

We were sitting there and studying and a fellow I had never seen eased on in the door.  People came and went all the time in Slana whether it was in service or in the home, they just sort of melted in and melted out and didn't bother with all the hellos and how do you do and everything.  They just stayed for what they were able to stay for and when they had other things to do they would go and do those.

Well, he slid in the door and he looked around and I could see he wasn't really thrilled with seeing the crowd that was in there.  You could tell he felt the pressure.  In a couple of minutes he eased on out.  I didn't know if he had something special on his mind or was just looking for somebody or what.  Nobody gave any sign that we needed to address him for anything.

So a few minutes later he came back in and he eased his parka down off his shoulders which was the way you do when you're inside and you're going to be inside for a little while but you can't really stay.  You don't take the parka off, but you get it off your shoulders and let some of the body heat get out so you don't get sweaty in the warm house or warm cabin and get real cold when you get outside because you're wet.

But he was there 12 to 14 minutes maybe.  He shrugged his shoulders, pulled that parka up and eased on out again.  Twenty minutes later he came back in.  I felt like we needed to somehow acknowledge this guy, so I said, "Hey, I'm Al Pearce, can I help you with something?"  He gave me his name, which unfortunately has gone out of my head, but I know his last name was Belt.  He said, "I read a page of the Old Testament every day, a page of the New Testament every day and I love Jesus." He said it just as fast as he could and then he sighed. You could tell that that was the announcement he had come for.

I said, "I'm sure glad to hear that and we're glad to have you at the Bible study. Please hang around and we'll get a chance to talk a little bit when we get this lesson done." The lesson finished up and people drifted out. He had gone outside, but he came back in when it was just Don, Wanda, him and me left in the cabin. He knew Don and Wanda real well. He was a true hermit. He had been in the service and he had some kind of a pension coming. I don't know whether it was military or from another job later on. He didn't like to be around people, but he got acquainted with Don and Wanda, which was real easy to do if you lived in Slana because they helped everybody and knew everybody and cared about everybody.

He got them to pick up his mail every Tuesday and Thursday and just keep it there at the house. He would then come by and pick it up from them and have a cup of coffee with them and bring them a piece of meat if he had had any luck or whatever. They became friends. In their friendship, Don and Wanda talked to him about the Lord.

One night in that cabin he had accepted Jesus Christ as his Savior and asked Jesus to come into his life. He was still a hermit but as time went on someone told him if you confess me before men I'll confess you before the Father. He felt like he had to make a public confession of Jesus Christ as his Savior. It was almost like it was necessary for salvation, which it's not. Your necessity for your salvation is God's grace and asking for forgiveness of your sins at one point in time and asking Jesus into your life.

In his mind it had to be done for some reason. He had come on a Tuesday afternoon for the purpose of making a public profession that Jesus Christ was his Savior. We got to talking and I told him that I had just come from Columbia, South Carolina. He said, "Well, that's really something." He said, "I had a cousin, we were in the Army together, and after we got out we'd write. We'd only write about once a month, but we sort of kept track because we were both only children and didn't have anybody else." And he gave me the date, I forget what it was, it was close to a year ago. "I wrote him a letter and it never came back, but he never sent me another one so I didn't write again and I don't know what happened to him. He was a pharmacist in a little family owned drug store out on Main Street in Columbia." I got to thinking and I said, "His name was Belt?" He said, "Yes, his name was Belt, B-E-L-T."

It just so happened that I had to respond to that drugstore in my duties as a deputy sheriff for Richland County the day that Mr. Belt had been shot and killed in a robbery at the store, before I had gone to the mission field. So the Lord sent me as a messenger to tell Mr. Belt what happened to his cousin and also to share with him in his grief, but also his joy because he knew his cousin knew the Lord. In fact, his cousin talked to him about the Lord many times, but he hadn't made a decision until just a short time before I met him there in Alaska.

God has his way of doing things. I am so thankful that He's got the whole big picture. He's got the whole world in His hands, and I'm thankful that He's got me in His hands. I wouldn't want to travel without Him. It's hard when you have to do a death notification to a family member. It's especially hard when it's a year later and the man has no idea it's coming. God was good and we were able to share in the joy of eternal life; rejoicing that cousins were going to be back together again with Jesus.

God bless you all. I trust that you will also find Jesus Christ as your Savior and that we'll be able to fellowship together in that eternal home

# CHAPTER THIRTY-FOUR

# MOST ANTI-SOCIAL MAN I EVER MET

Missionary responsibilities are varied in Alaska. When you're in the bush it takes about 50 percent of the time just to live and the rest of the time you try to do ministry. It takes so long to live you've got to do lifestyle evangelism. There are very few hours that you get to preach and teach; most of the time you're one-on-one.

Missionaries sort of belong to everybody and if somebody had a special need he was the one you went to. It was great because we had opportunities to share God's love and just material things, giving somebody a ride somewhere, making a special contact carrying a message or whatever because of the lifestyle that we lived there.

There was a fellow who was an extreme recluse and he lived about three miles off Nebesna Road. He just didn't care to be around people at all. So much so that he had the mailman actually on his bank account and the mailman would take care of his shopping and everything such as cashing his pension check, and buying his supplies. A mailman is sort of like a missionary in Alaska. He has a lot of varied functions besides that one assigned by the U.S. Post Office.

Anyway, old Ed Buren, who has now passed on, was a friend of mine and he was the mailman.

He came to me one day and he said, Preacher, there's a fellow that I do all these things for, he just doesn't like to come out from the bush; he doesn't want to be around people.  He's real sick.  He did get out to the box to leave me a note to get some sort of medicine for him and I left the medicine and it is still in the box and has been there a couple of days.

Somebody, and I knew who that somebody was in his mind, somebody needs to go check on him to see if he's all right.

Well, I told him that it was wintertime and I'd get the old Sherpa snowshoes.  I had some of those wooden man killers early on that were old Army surplus and they about beat me to death, but somehow -- I can't remember the story behind them now -- I ended up with a pair of Sherpas that fit me.  They were light-weight aluminum webbing and a whole lot more comfortable.  I could make three miles an hour in them.

So going back to the cabin I figured I had an hour each way, plus whatever time I had back there, so I started early in the day.  Like I said, it was wintertime.  I don't recall exactly what time of the month.  We probably had six hours daylight.  So I started.  I parked at his mailbox on Nebesna Road just about the time it got light and started walking.  It was probably 30 or 35 below.  It was cold, but I had seen colder.

I got in there and got back to the cabin and knocked on the door.  I didn't get a response.  Of course, I didn't know if the guy I was coming to check on was dead or alive, so after an hour's hike on the shoes I unstrapped the snowshoes and opened the door.  As I stepped in the cabin, the old fellow was sitting there by the table looking at me and he was alive.  I said, "Hello there, I'm Al Pearce."  Before I could say anything else he said, "I know exactly who you are." He said, "But let me tell you one thing, I'd rather have aids than company." Try and figure a real quick answer to that one. That's sort of like you're not welcome in my house and neither is anybody else.

Anyway, I told him, "You know who I am; you know where I am and if you ever need me you're welcome. Jesus loves you and I'll get out of your way." He didn't say another word. I just stepped out and put shoes on and headed back. I was gone from the road about two hours and seven or eight minutes. It was two hours of walking in snowshoes and seven minutes of one-sided conversation.

I don't recall his name either. Of course, most of the things are gone now. I should have started writing this book 15 years ago like my Daddy told me, but it didn't happen that way. I don't know what happened to him. The mailman has passed away now too, so I don't have a clue. I haven't found out anything about him but, again, God knows. I hope that at some time he knew that Jesus loved him and he was willing to let Jesus into his life even though he wasn't going to let humans in.

## CHAPTER THIRTY-FIVE

## "EGLICK"

The native people have a lot of their own ways and many of them are good ways, many of them are precious, and they're kind to people. One of the interesting things is there are only a few words left of the Athabascan language that the majority of people would recognize or be able to say. One of them is "eglick" and it means bad luck overtook him.

Now, when you're there in the native country and somebody gets shot in a hunting accident, he got shot in a hunting accident. If he got mauled by a bear, he got mauled by a bear. You know, they just spell it out. But if for some reason that person took his own life, "eglick" bad luck overtook him.

The natives felt like if you said that a person committed suicide you would endanger their eternal destiny; in fact, you would condemn them to hell.

By God's grace we know we're saved by His grace. We live by His grace. And if for whatever reason we die a premature death, as men see it, we're still saved by His grace and saved for all eternity.

I'm so glad I'm a part of the family of God because God never puts anybody out of His family. And even "eglick" won't take me away from Him. God bless you all.

## CHAPTER THIRTY-SIX

# SHANAN

Another word that many Christians recognize in the Athabascan language is "shanan". When Christians meet they often greet each other with shanan and the other will respond shanan nochtane. Shanan, praise God, thank God. The natives themselves can say it with such inflection that they can define which one they're saying. White men can't pick up the difference. They say that they just put both meanings on it for us because it's the only way they could present it.

Shanan nochtane means I too praise the Lord. So it's a common greeting; it's a common exclamation of true praise to our Father in heaven who cares for us and provides us blessing. The Athabascans say that their national anthem is *Amazing Grace*. You may recall some people, for the last verse of *Amazing Grace,* sing: Praise God, praise God, praise God, praise God. The Athabascans sing: shanan, shanan, shanan nochtane, shanan nochtane, shanan; Shanan nochtane, shanan nochtane, shanan nochtane, shanan.

Amazing grace that God allows us to cross language barriers, receive the blessings of wonderful words that fellow Christians say and we can rejoice with them. I thank God for my friends, for my native friends, for each of you. Shanan.

## CHAPTER THIRTY-SEVEN

## LAST FLIGHT IN ALASKA

When it came time to leave Alaska I was going to be driving a 1973 international school bus which became an object of comedy before it was all over. It was inadvisable to drive down the Alaskan highway alone in a big vehicle. Lou Riddley, an old friend from Columbia, decided to fly to Alaska and help me drive out.

Lou was a commercial driving instructor and able to drive just about anything on tracks or wheels, so he was a real handy fellow to have and he was real adept at teaching me to drive this school bus with the two-speed axle and the five-speed transmission.

That gets on to the next story. Lou was a friend from flying days in Richland County when I was the aircraft commander in charge of the aviation division of the Richland County Sheriff's Department. Lou loved to fly and he literally loved to fly anything. Still does. He flies everything from a CESNA Citation Jet to antique Tail Dragger open cockpit bi-planes. If it flies, he loves it. If it moves on wheels or tracks he loves it and he's real good company when you're dealing with those things.

I had a friend who had a CESNA 170, which was one of the chapters in this book you've probably already read. He told me that I could borrow it and take Lou flying when he arrived in Alaska. He'd come in to Anchorage in an airliner, but he'd been asleep and he had missed a lot of scenery. Driving up through the Alaska Range, through the Wrangell Mountains, he saw a lot of the country, but he hadn't been in the air yet.

So I got him in the left seat of that Cessna 170 and we took off. I had him turn left and then go down into the Copper River valley, which is like a canyon. It's quite deep. You can actually take off and in a half a mile you can go 200 feet below the airport elevation and fly following the river. In that 170, which is very responsive, it was fun to do. I kept him down there flying that. Then there is a point going up towards, Nebesna where the valley starts to fan out and you get more open country.

I got him going full throttle there and just as fast as that CESNA 170 would go, and I told him to pull back in a zoom climb and just pull it up until it's almost in a stall, get all the altitude you can. And he hauls back on it and the nose came up and, of course, all you see is the nose of that airplane. He got up about 300 feet and was almost in a stall and slow flight and I said, "Push the nose over and look." He did, and he was looking at the Wrangell Mountains. He did a slow 360 degree turn and looked at every point on the compass. He was looking at the mountains, the Wrangells, the Alaska Range; the Chugach Mountains. It was awesome.

Lou really enjoyed that flight. It was the only flight that he and I were able to make together in Alaska, but it was a lot of fun to see him pop up out of that valley and then shove the nose over on that airplane and look. His eyes were as big as silver dollars, as he saw the vast expanse of Alaska and what God had made there. It's just beautiful country. It was a fun day before we had to start loading the school bus and heading out. That's the next chapter.

# CHAPTER THIRTY-EIGHT

## LEAVING OUT

You've already heard about the 1973 international school bus which probably had a million miles on it, I don't know. It was pretty well worn out, but we just did what we had to do. A number of people helped us load it leaving, but when it got down to the little stuff, once all the heavy furniture, tools and everything were loaded, Lou and I did the rest.

I wasn't happy to be leaving. I probably wasn't the best company in the world and I thank God that Lou hung around. I think he probably would have hitchhiked back to Anchorage and flown out if he had known what we were going to have to go through, but we went through it together, we went through it as a team and we had a lot of fun. But there were a lot of sad moments.

One of my customs that my father taught me early on in life was when you set out on a trip you take time to talk to the Lord about it and ask Him to watch over you and use you for His service along the way. I didn't want to pull out of the parking lot at Chistochina. The parsonage was actually right on the back side of the parking lot of the chapel. I didn't want to pull out of there without praying and I was so distraught I wasn't even able to pray. On that occasion Lou took the lead, and I believe that's the first time I heard Lou pray out loud, but he asked the Lord for grace to get us through and especially interceded on my behalf because he knew how messed up I was mentally and physically. I was tired because I wasn't resting as things were.

We started out, got that thing in gear, and off we went heading towards Slana. The group at Slana was there for their service time on Sunday afternoon. Of course, the chapel building was gone, but they still met on that location in good weather, looking toward the day when God would raise up a building.

Little Wanda led the group and said we're going to lay our hands on this bus and pray that God will take them through. It was ironic, she laid her hand on the right front tire of the bus, some of the little kids ran around and laid their hands on the left front tire, and a few more went back and laid their hands on the right rear and they asked God to just carry us through and keep us safe and use us in His service wherever we were and provide for our needs. It was a wonderful prayer of dedication for the trip.

We got in after hugs and tears. I was going to drive that first part. I got that thing going. Keep in mind that it was a 5-speed transmission with a two-speed axle, so I didn't have twin sticks. As the truck driver said, I just had the one shift lever and a button. I was not an accomplished commercial driver by any means, but Lou actually taught for the commercial driver's license and was very familiar. One of the other things he had done was drive a truck and heavy equipment and could move about anything on wheels or tracks that he decided to move.

But since I was familiar with the road, I was going to drive the first part. We got out, headed up, and got up above Duffy's Tavern at mile 58. It was a struggle because we were starting half way up the hill and loaded as heavy as we were couldn't get above third gear on the low side of the axle. So we went up that hill at about 26 or 28 miles an hour I guess. We got in the flat and I wound it up and we were going well. We were probably up to about 50 or 55 because we had a straightaway and a downhill. Boom, left rear tire blew out. Now, keep in mind we're all of 26 miles out on a 4,200 mile trip when we blew the first tire.

Well, we had a compressor. Of course, they had split rims so we could jack it up and put the inside wheel on a block for safety and we pulled the outside, because only the outside tire blew. We pulled it off and put a new tube and a new tire on it, pumped it up with an air tank. The cigarette lighter operated the compressor, which took forever. Well, right about the time we were tightening the lugs, putting it back on, the bus shifted a little bit, just enough to break the jack. So now we're in a rattling old bus, loaded real heavy, blown the first tire, 26 miles out on the trip and we don't have a jack.

So off we went. We got to Tok before we had the next problem. Tok was 92 miles. We were about 86 or 88 miles into the trip when we blew another one. It was the inside left tire. We blew it right near Fellows, a little mom and pop tire shop. It just so happened he had a couple of 920 tires. This was not the 1020 that everybody runs and you can find anywhere at any truck stop, these were 920, which were not real common. He had a couple of 920 tires and tubes and a jack for sale. It was a bigger, heavier jack than what we had. I think it

was a six-ton that he sold us, or it might even have been an eight-ton.
So we mounted the tires that he sold us and had two new tires on the left rear now.

We started to go down the road and I passed the intersection of the Tok cutoff that went back to Glennallen, back to Chistochina, heading down towards Northway, towards the Canadian border. Lou said, "Hey Al, hang a right there." I said, "Man, that's backtracking. That goes back to Chistochina." He said, "I know." He said, "We need to go back to that church and let those people lay hands on the left rear wheel too; that's the only one they didn't touch and pray over and that's the only one that went flat."

Lou's sense of humor was great. He kept me going. Many times I was laughing so hard I was crying and other times I was crying and he'd get me laughing. He was a good traveling companion.

We started on down the road and when we got to customs they just looked at it. Keep in mind, Lou had finished up repacking, filling in the slots, and he had done a few artistic things. I was bringing the caribou rack that had been on the tongue of the mobile home that we lived in. Somebody had left it, I believe it was Joe Virgin, and they told me I could have it. It was a good sized rack. I was also bringing my moose rack, the one from the moose I had shot when I was up there. Lou decided to mount these two sets of horns so it appeared like we had a cross between a moose and a caribou riding on the top of the bus. The customs agent just cracked up. He waived us on through. He looked probably two, three minutes, and I guess he decided if there was anything in there dangerous we probably couldn't find it anyway before we got through Canada so he just sent us on our way.

We started on down the Alaska Highway. Life is interesting on the Alaska Highway. That year was a particularly hard year because they had a lot of mud slides. They didn't necessarily have the best markings, detours or roadblocks. We came around a turn at a pretty good clip and all of a sudden there was a bulldozer in the middle of the road pushing about four feet of mud that had slid down off the side of the mountain. Lou just started grabbing gears and he pulled it down. We were in mud a foot deep. We didn't dare stop. If we stopped we'd never get this thing started again as loaded and as heavy as it was.

He kept going down to the next gear, whatever it took to keep it moving, and he finally got to the low gear on the low side of the axle, which gave us a top speed of probably four to five miles an hour. He held it clear to the floor and it just kept turning and pulling and moving, but it was a crawl. He'd ease up a little bit trying to see if the wheels would catch and give us good traction so that we would move at the same rate that the wheel was turning, but it wouldn't. It just kept sliding or bogging.

So he held it clear to the floor and it was somewhere about an hour and 15 minutes before we got through that mudslide. Of course, we couldn't swap drivers. Occasionally his foot would get so tired I would sit down on the steps of the old school bus and hold the accelerator all the way down with my hand while he'd flex his ankle and shift his leg around and everything. I did pretty well as a cruise control, but he didn't want to do that on a regular basis.

As we got through that and moved on of course we had burned a lot of fuel. The average for the whole trip was eight miles to the gallon, but when you take an hour and a half to go three or four miles at full throttle you burn a lot of fuel. So the next problem was to get some fuel. We hadn't been able to really plan the fuel stops. We did have a couple of containers, five-gallon containers of fuel that we could pour in if we needed it, but we were trying to keep that for reserve.

We moved on, got fueled up and changed over and I was driving. We hadn't gone too far along and going up a hill I shifted, and keep in mind Lou, the ever present instructor in the truck driving school was coaching me, and I did exactly what he told me. I was so glad that he was alert and had me doing exactly what I was supposed to do. As I shifted gears, the clutch blew up. I mean blew up.

We had to get towed into Whitehorse, Yukon Territory. That was an experience all by itself. I don't remember what it cost. It was a bundle because they had to use the big wrecker like they used for pulling a semi. They got us in. There was nobody who could really work on the bus at the time, but we had a friend, David Gotlob, a missionary friend of mine who was stationed in Whitehorse. He knew a fellow who had a garage, but he said he was so busy right at the time with some other things he wasn't able to fix it, but he would allow us to use his rack to jack the bus up and we could pull the transmission, use his transmission jack and all that to pull it out and put the clutch in.

So we started, and it was not an easy project. This bus had not been well maintained for a long time. It was rusty and outside of the rust was a good coat of grease and oil and junk that prevented us from doing anything real quick. We had to soak and clean and scrub and wire brush to get down to nuts and bolts and then had to work on them with an impact tool, which the fellow loaned us.

When we completed that part and got the transmission out, pulled the bell housing, the clutch came out in five or six pieces. Well, that's not good. It's supposed to be one, big nice round piece. But it was a bunch of little jagged pieces. We put them back together to match them up, to measure it, and we found out it was a nine-inch clutch, which was extremely unusual. They all had 11 or 12-inch clutches – but here we were with the off-the-wall, strange, illegitimate child of somebody's mechanics in Alaska.

We took the pieces up to the only parts store that was open at that particular time, and it was now late in the evening, though it was summertime in the Yukon and still bright, plenty of sunlight we could work with, but every place was fixing to close. We went in and showed them what we had and gave them serial numbers. According to the serial numbers it should have been the standard sized clutch and it wasn't, but we had no way of converting it to the standard sized clutch because the bell housing and the linkage had all been changed over.

The guy behind the counter said he'd order us one. He could have it flown in but it's probably going to take a few days because it's going to have to come from somewhere down in the United States and there's not much he can do. It's just non-standard and he hadn't seen one of them in years.

Well, it just so happened about that time, a fellow who had been a mechanic and had retired and come back and spent a little time working around the place as the janitor and helped organize some parts and just keep things going to give him something to do and sort of help the old company a little bit, pushed his broom up there and he leaned on the broom and he looked and he said, "That's a nine-inch clutch, isn't it?" The clerk said, "Yeah, it's a nine-inch clutch. Have you seen one of them lately?" He said, "Yep. I've been moving one for a couple of years. It's back here in the back and I've got to sweep around it all the time, so you might as well sell it to them and I won't have to sweep around it no more."

He went back and brought this brand new clutch in an old raggedy beat up box because it had been kicked around, rain had leaked in the window and the box had all come apart, but here was a brand new clutch. So we picked it up in our grimy little claws, headed back to the shop, put it all back together, cranked it up and drove it off of that pit, the rack which had a pit under it where we could work with the jack. We made sure it worked.

We went back to Dave and Cathy Gotlob's for a cleanup time. Cathy, in her usual fashion, fed us well. Cathy is a great cook. We had a good dinner, slept for a while, and got up early the next morning and off we went again down the Alaska Highway. We call it the ALCAN; the Canadians call it the Alaska Highway. They don't take any responsibility for it. They say it's something the United States did. It was an interesting cross-cultural experience, believe me.

As was custom, my shift of driving was the first shift of the day. I got to driving and things were going pretty well. All these things may not be in perfect chronological order because I've lost the diary that I made of that trip. Anyway, I had driven a good bit and I'd gotten tired. Of course, I was pretty depressed anyway, so it was easy for me to tell Lou he could drive. He loved to drive and was good at it.

Lou got behind the wheel. There was one seat behind the driver's seat where we had room to sit. You couldn't really lie down, you just sort of leaned back. It was a short school bus seat. I had a pillow against the window and I was laying back going to sleep and, in fact, had gone to sleep and was probably sleeping very comfortably all things considered. We were going down the mountain at a good rate of speed and there was a rock wall right beside us. For whatever reason, someone had replaced the standard old school bus door with a wooden one. It looked like a screen door to an old cabin that had been cut to fit, and then they put some Plexiglas in it and it was held closed with a deadbolt lock. Whenever you got out of it, you put a padlock on the outside to lock it. But with enough vibration the deadbolt lock had shifted, and as it came loose the door popped open into the wind stream and broke.

If you've ever heard an old international truck pulling up a hill and then start downhill and get it wound up and everything is going good and you're really at high speed, you know, 55 or 60 miles an hour, which is fast for that thing, and it's screaming and we've got this wonderful wall that all the noise reverberates off and poof, the door that's keeping that noise out is gone…I was wide awake hanging on to everything, trying desperately to make sure that we didn't have any other major problems that only the laundry lady could solve.

Lou got tickled. He got it slowed down and he got it stopped, but he laughed and laughed and laughed. I had to fix that door by myself because he couldn't quit laughing. He said he had never seen anyone come from a semi-reclining position, eyes shut, to completely erect grabbing, grasping, eyes as big as watermelons in a split second, and he just thought it was the funniest thing he'd seen in a long time.

Now, it was a while before I appreciated his humor. After we got the door put back together and got it locked up so that we could use it to lock the bus when we needed to or just to keep the rain and the wind and the noise out a little bit while we were traveling, I started to see his humor.

We logged every fuel stop and kept careful track of the mileage because we had long stretches in Canada where we could not get gas or fuel of any type, and we needed to be able to calculate whether we could make the next one or would have to get some more five-gallon containers.

We went into Watson Lake running low and decided that we were just going to have to bite the bullet and fill up. Watson Lake is usually the most expensive point on the Alaska Highway. They're so far from anybody else they know you just about have to buy fuel there and they know everybody bought minimum fuel there, so they jacked up the price and got the most they could.

Now, keep in mind this is in June of 1991 that we're moving and we're buying imperial gallons, as the Canadians sell it. We did our calculations and near as we could figure out, in actual U.S. gallons we were probably paying about $3.75 a gallon for regular gas at that time. We thought that was very expensive. I guess everybody was paying $1.10 anywhere else, so they got their share and they got their transportation fee and everybody went through.

Just a side note, if you ever do decide to go up the Alaska Highway or the ALCAN to drive it, get yourself a copy of the current <u>Mile Post</u>. It has the listings of every service available along the road, and the comparative costs. You'll know where to stop and take on all the fuel you can and you'll know where to just get your minimum so that you can get to the next point and it'll help you calculate how much you'll need to get to your next point. It's got all kinds of charts in it. It's a really handy book and it's very well done. I haven't looked for one in a long time. I hope they're still around. They're certainly a great aid as you travel the Alaska Highway.

Anyway, back to the story. We were going on and stopped to get fuel at another old gas station. It was just a gas station and a restroom and not much else and there was a good bit of graffiti on the walls.

I don't even think they had a Coke machine. One of the poems, and I can't recite it fully but I got a kick out of it, talked about the ALCAN and the shape it was in. It said the way this road is laid out it's hard to tell whether the lout that built the road was going to hell or leaving out.

The ALCAN is a gravel road. Now, I was born and raised in Illinois. I know pea gravel and I'm familiar with the larger gravel, but Canadian gravel is about the size of your fist. These semi-trucks, particularly tankers, run up and down it at 75, 80 miles an hour and they sling up these rocks that are a little bigger than tennis balls. Everybody that travels the ALCAN just anticipates putting in a new windshield by the end of the trip.

Our windshield was good. We didn't lose a windshield on the bus. I guess it was higher up, and maybe the Lord knew we had enough other problems we didn't need to be riding open air when that windshield came in.

All of a sudden there was a noise that didn't make a bit of sense and then it sounded like we had no exhaust system whatsoever, like it was just spitting straight out straight pipes. We got it on up the hill because to stop on the hill with all that weight you would never get it moving again at any kind of pace. We got to the top of the hill and got out, opened the hood and guess what? We were running straight pipes right at the manifold. The pipe had blown out. I don't know whether it backfired and we didn't hear it or what, but a very, very corroded, rusted exhaust pipe had disintegrated and left about a four-inch stub. That's really loud in a V-8 engine.

We were going into Fort Nelson and it was probably 20 after four in the afternoon. Canadians are good about their closing time. I don't know how they open up, whether it's on time or not, but closing time is 5 o'clock and they pretty well close up at closing time.

We're easing into this village trying to not sound like an Army tank invading and we could see a van ahead with blue lights on it and knew it was a Canadian mounted police who are the only people you see policing on the Alaska Highway. We decided we'd just hang a right and try one of the side streets of the village and just see what we could come up with, at least find a payphone and a phonebook.

Wouldn't you know it, it just so happened that as we turned right and went down about three streets and turned left on what looked like a pretty well traveled divider street, the first building we come to is an exhaust shop. I asked the guy if he had a new exhaust system for a 1973 International school bus. His humor was worse than Lou's. He just had all kinds of things to say about that, but by the time he got done slapping his knee and laughing and carrying on and telling all his help that, hey, they think there are actually extra pieces for that thing lying around the countryside, that old dinosaur, he sat down and said that for a very reasonable fee, and I forget what it was, $25 or $30, he said, "If you'll get that piece of the straight pipes off of the manifold and you get the other piece loose I'll fabricate...I'll have to use the stub pipe because I don't have a flange to fit it, but I'll fabricate you a new exhaust system. But I've got to be finished by 5 o'clock because I close at five. You're welcome to leave it parked on my property tonight and I'll get it in the morning when I open up or have it in my hands so that I can finish by five."

Well, we asked him how long it would take for him to do his part and he said, "oh, about 15 minutes."

So Lou and I skedaddled and I got under there and I was trying my best with a few tools we borrowed from him. We got the nuts loose, but we couldn't get the thing out. I skinned my knuckles and burned my hand, and several other things were worn thin too. Lou said to let him try, so I got out of the way. And as he tried and it just wasn't coming, we were now up to 20 minutes to five, so basically we've got five minutes or all night.

Well, I got irate. I grabbed him by the feet, slid him out from under there on that creeper, and I thought the creeper was part of the problem because every time we'd try and pull on it the creeper would roll and bop around and we couldn't get a hold of things.

I crawled under there and I went to yanking and snatching and grabbing and pulling and I guess I had discussed some of its problems and Lou said, "Come on preacher now, we've got to be more careful here." Well, right about that time it turned loose and I slung the piece out. Lou grabbed the other piece and ran up there and the guy welded us a new exhaust system.

But true to form, at about three minutes to five he handed it to us and he stayed long enough to write a bill. He left us sitting on the curb right beside his business with a real nice shiny homemade exhaust system and he went home. It took us a little while but we did it together.

By then we'd been on the road about six days. We hadn't stayed in a motel or had a warm shower since we left Whitehorse and the Gotlobs' hospitality. So we sprung for a motel that night and had a real nice dinner at a sit-down restaurant after we had a warm shower. We then went home and crawled under the sheets and slept there instead of on the floor of the bus and on that stubby seat. We had a good time. Lou said we ought to go see a movie, but there wasn't a movie in that particular town, but it was sort of a fun laid back time and we regrouped a little bit.

Well, come the next morning we were up and rolling at about 7:30 or 8 o'clock, fairly early, got down the road a little ways and had a breakfast. We were on the road again and we had used all of our spare tires. Nobody had 920's, everybody had 1020's. So every time we got near a place that might have some, we'd stop and ask them if they had any 920's. We blew the outside left rear again. I probably should have listened to Lou; I probably should have gone back to Slana and let them bless that one too, but we didn't.

We pulled up into this little tire shop and the guy looked at it and said, "You've got 920's on that?" I said, "Yes, sir, I do." He said, "Well, I've got one brand new one and two used ones that I've been trying to get rid of. If you take them all I'll give you a deal." Well, we were into deals. We were probably less than halfway and we figured that we were probably going to use at least several more before we finished that road. So he jacked it up with his hydraulic jack and changed the tire out and we didn't even have to get greasy on that one, and we took the two spares and tied them up on top ready to go and got two new tubes. Off we went down the road again.

Well, about this time we crossed the Canadian border, and when we crossed and came into the United States, the custom agent looked at it and just shook his head. Of course, the caribou and moose racks are still riding in their pristine positions looking like some kind of a weird Neanderthal animal.

He asked us, "How did you ever get through the Canadian vehicle inspection stations?" We said, "We didn't know anything about them." He said, "When you drive anything through Canada that has more than four wheels, and keep in mind the school bus had six, you're required to stop at these government inspection points for safety inspection and security to make sure the vehicle is safe to travel in Canada and won't be broken down alongside the highway somewhere and it won't endanger any Canadians." Oops. Nobody ever told us about that and we drove right by a bunch of them and none of them flagged us down. Of course, we might have looked like a bunch of gypsies that they really didn't want to deal with anyway. I'm sure that we probably looked like a dangerous group.

But we headed on through and we got to a point where I thought things were going to get more interesting. I had often heard of Great Falls, Montana, and here we were, heading into Great Falls. Well, Lou was running short on his vacation time and wanted to get to his cousin or his nephew's wedding back in New York, so he was going to stay overnight there in Great Falls and the next morning as we started out, I was going to drive him to the airport and he was going to fly out and head to the wedding. Well, it didn't work that way. It started to work that way.

We stayed overnight at a real nice motel, I think it was Holiday Inn, it was about the only thing in town. We had a nice time. We watched TV that night. We just relaxed, chilled out and had fun. The next morning Lou had to be at the airport at about 9 o'clock. Lou said, "We get up, you get me to the airport about 8 o'clock so I can check in, get my flight and all." He said, "I figure you need a day's rest before you start any further. At least you're in the United States now. I'm going to pay for an extra night at a motel. You just come back here, chill out all day and take it easy. This is your day of rest for the week and tomorrow morning you start out and just be careful on the road and I'll be praying for you."

I hated to see the old boy go. He sure was good company and handy to have around. Well, as the Lord would have it, I got him up there and I started back. He was processing in and I was going to go eat. He was going to have breakfast on the airplane and I decided I was going to go get some breakfast. Maybe I'd just walk to the little restaurant across the street and I'd park the school bus in the motel parking lot. This thing wasn't fun to travel around in in small towns and on small roads. It was about as handy as a hippopotamus when you tried to move in small quarters.

Coming down the hill, they had one red light in town and it is right at the bottom of the hill, there's a fairly busy crossroad. I got to catching gears, shifting down, trying to save the brakes and it was picking up speed. I shifted another gear down and it was still picking up speed. I hit the brakes and the pedal went clear to the floor. Well, I wanted to start singing "Lord I'm coming home," but I didn't. I pumped and nothing happened. I knew the emergency brake wasn't much of an option in this situation, so I started double clutching and shifting and pulling and I finally got it slowed down.

I heard this terrible clatter out of the engine. Well, I got it down, went through the red light and hung a right and got into the motel parking lot. I truly hoped at that particular time right turn on red was authorized, but as the pilots would say it was an emergency situation so I had a right to deviate from standard procedure because that thing wasn't going to stop. I got it in there and it sounded like it was chugging on about three cylinders. I knew this was not good. So far we had a door blow out, we had tires blow out, we had a number of other various things happen, including the exhaust system, but now the engine.

I didn't even have the energy to go get breakfast. I just went up, decided I was going to chill out for an hour or two and think about this thing and get my head together before I started anything. I was in the bathroom and I heard the door open. Well, I figured it was the cleaning lady and I hollered "it's okay". By the time I got out of the bathroom there was Lou. His flight was booked solid, he couldn't leave. He had got a ride back. I don't know how he got a ride back at the end of the world there. I'm sure there weren't any taxis. But he got the key from the desk. I hugged him so much I think he was worried that I had changed my sexual preference. He looked like an angel in disguise. It was a good disguise, but he was an angel in disguise.

We started out and naturally we let our fingers do the walking, so we started with the Yellow Pages. Now, let me tell you, if you want to go to Great Falls go right ahead, but don't go on the weekend because it's closed. We got answering machines that said call back Monday morning after nine. We got rude people that said they were just a cleanup man and there isn't nobody here that works on anything, leave me alone. We tried everything in the book and there wasn't anything.

So we eased on down and asked the desk clerk who around here fixes things? He said, "The only person in town is that fellow at the gas station across the street and they don't work on anything but regular oil changes and all, but they close at noon on Saturday. He does work out in the alley behind the station on his own, which they authorize." I would have tried him, but this didn't sound like the greatest place to get an engine rebuilt behind a gas station in the alley right next to the Chinese restaurant.

They told us of a guy just over the mountain about 18 or 20 miles, so we tried to run it over the mountain and it wasn't pulling but on maybe three cylinders and it wasn't going to go. So we had to ease it back and turned around and went back. We walked in and talked to the guy in the filling station and he said, "Yeah." He said, "I can fix anything if my daddy tells me what's wrong with it." The fellow's name was John Peterson. He was a big old lanky fellow. He had been in the Air Force and for whatever reason he had gotten out. His daddy was a brilliant mechanic, could diagnose and troubleshoot anything. John was just more hands on and as long as his daddy told him what the problem was he could fix it.

Well, I could see this coming. You know, here I go. I'm going to pay $50 an hour for a mechanic and $100 an hour for a counselor and advisor and this thing is going to get expensive, but when you're sitting there with all your worldly possessions on six wheels and you're down in a valley and it won't go over the mountain either way, you don't have a lot of choice. So I went to check and I asked him, "Where's your daddy"? He said, "In the bar there across the street."

So he went over there and got his daddy. His daddy came over and said crank it up. We cranked it up. He told John a couple things to do and John did them. He said, "Well, you've got a couple bent push rods and you've probably got at least one busted and maybe two, but you're right it's running on about three cylinders and it's not going to go over the mountain."

So I asked him what the chances were of getting the parts and getting it on the road today. I think he had to go about 60 miles to get parts over the mountain. He said he could get them, but he's got a pickup truck and there's only room for two and all I had was traveler's checks and a credit card. I was going to have to give him some kind of money. I seriously wondered about just handing my credit card to a person I didn't know, but he seemed honest and I figured I'd try him. So I gave it to him.

John pulled the heads real quick and looked at it, the heads were all right, didn't need to get the heads done, but needed a full gasket set and he pulled out four bent push rods and two broken ones. He headed out to get them. I asked him how much a whole set of 16 new push rods would cost, since obviously these had gone many, many miles and many, many moons. They were probably original equipment. He got a whole set and he came back and put that thing together in record time. He cranked it up and it purred like a kitten.

So I asked him if he had had anything to eat and he hadn't eaten much. He drank a number of warm Coors that he loaded onto his toolbox when he brought it out from the station. I don't know, I think he thought water was for washing and he hadn't drunk it in a long time, but he was a good boy and he was still stone-cold sober even though he'd drunk a good many beers.

We got together and asked if he wanted to go to the Chinese restaurant. He said, "Well, I've never eaten there." I thought well, that's a nice way to treat him and sort of soften him up, you know. A lot of times a man's bill is not near as bad if he ain't hungry, so we took him in and bought him a meal and we had a good time. He was just a real fine man to be around. He was very positive, very friendly and very efficient.

We needed some ice, but they didn't have any so we were going down to K-Mart to get a bag of ice to throw in our cooler and put a few groceries in because from now on it was going to be sandwiches and sodas out of the cooler. The money was running extremely low. We went down to K-Mart and asked him if there was anything he wanted. He said, "Well, I've always wanted a torque wrench, but I've never had one." Well, they had torque wrenches and we got him a torque wrench and gave him that. We gave him a ride in our wonderful old dinosaur.

We came back to the station and he put his tools away. We said, "Okay John, the moment of truth, you know, what's it going to cost?" And he looked at me with sort of a blank look and he said, "Nothing. I just like to help people." I was really feeling a tinge of guilt since I was afraid the way he was doing everything he was going to just jack up the bill and take about half of my life savings and my first born just to get that bus on the road. He had no intentions of charging me anything.

I said, "Well, let me give you something." He said, "No, I just like to help people. I said, "Well John, did you ever have somebody that you want to help and they didn't have money to buy the parts? He said, "Oh yeah. Yeah, that happens all the time out here. The economy is pretty bad out here." I said, "Well, let me give you a little bit of money and you just put it back until you run into somebody that needs parts they can't afford and then you use that to get the parts so you can help." He said, "Well, I could do that." And I'm sure if he hasn't run into somebody who needed money for parts by this time, it's probably tucked away in his wallet just waiting for the day when he could help somebody.

John was another angel in disguise. He was truly a generous, giving man. He gave of his time and his talents and didn't really expect anything back. God provided a good many of them along the way.

Off we went. We set out Sunday morning across the mountain after staying in the motel another night because it was already paid for. We watched movies and relaxed and had a good time. It was a wild part of the trip. The trip wasn't over yet. We still had another 1,200 miles to go or maybe farther.

Going into Minneapolis we had another blow out on the interstate or on the expressway. It was a few miles to a tire shop. They jacked it up but we'd used our new spare and we only had the two used spares and neither of them looked good. He just happened to have a brand new 920, so he put it on and we went on to the airport and got Lou on his flight heading out.

We set out into Minnesota and Lou grabbed a flight out of Minneapolis heading home. His vacation time had run out and he literally had to get off the plane, take a shower and go to work because he'd eaten all his vacation time just in his generosity in helping me.

I set out solo to Platteville, Wisconsin to take some well-earned rest with Mom and Dad. I was in Platteville when Lou was able to get in touch with some people who had contacted my wife and son. She called me there and basically told me that our life together was over. She did stop in after that and it was a hard time. She left and I had to go on and do two more speaking engagements. It was sort of a debriefing from the mission which had already been scheduled.

As soon as I finished that second one I resigned the mission because going into the divorce this would be an embarrassment to the mission and to the church. I didn't want to do that at that time.

Someone asked Lou Riddley what he thought of that trip and his comment was: "God just sent us across Alaska and Canada and down through the United States collecting the last available parts to a 1973 international school bus." Lou was one that really observed God's faithfulness in provisions through these hard times and was a good sport through the whole thing.

God is good. He brought me through that and a few more chapters will tell you more of the things He's done in the meantime. God bless you as you leave whatever comfortable point in your life that you may have liked, where you could do what you want, and then God rocks your boat and sends you out into something else. God is faithful. The purpose of this book is for you to see that.

## CHAPTER THIRTY-NINE

## I AM MY BROTHER'S KEEPER

If you've been reading this book you've figured out that I wasn't raised in the South and I'm not familiar with all of the problems related to the South. I'm a pretty happy go-lucky guy. Usually when I meet somebody, even people older than me if they're not a whole lot older, I'll say hey boy, how are you doing? To my preacher, Butch Morrison, who is just a month and a week older than me I'd say, Hey boy, how's it going today?

Well, one Sunday morning I shook hands with Robert Nelson who's in our church. He's a black brother; a precious brother in the Lord. He and his wife have added a lot to our church with their involvement, her music and so forth. I said, "Hey boy, how are you?" He came right up in my face and said, "I am a man." I never had any doubt about that. Robert played football for Georgia. He is in really good shape. There is no doubt about his physical prowess or anything in his spiritual life either.

I didn't realize how offensive it was to him. Some people raised in the South would never call him a man. They would call him boy and look down on him. That wasn't what I was intending. What I said was quite innocent, but it wasn't accepted that way, and I'm glad. It hurt me very much. Not that Robert came up in my face because he was completely right in doing so, but it hurt me that I said something that hurt my brother.

The Apostle Paul said, "If meat makes my brother to offend I will eat no meat while the world stands." Well, if the Apostle Paul can give up filet mignon I can certainly give up a few words, when I realize what they are, so that I don't say the wrong thing to the wrong people. Was I wrong to say to Robert, hey boy, how are you? No. There's nothing immoral about it and there's nothing in scripture that tells me I shouldn't have done that. Would I be wrong to say it again knowing that it hurt him? Yes. You see, I am my brother's keeper.

When you preach the gospel, a lot of times people are offended by the gospel. People are often offended by Jesus because of pride. They don't want to accept grace, they want to be good enough for salvation and Jesus, of course, says they're not.

Be careful. Make sure the offense is the gospel whether you're preaching or living the Christian life. Don't be the offense yourself. Sometimes we suffer persecution for the gospel's sake and sometimes we suffer it because we've brought it on ourselves. We need to be careful. When God asked Cain, where is your brother, Cain answered God with a question: "Am I my brother's keeper?"

The Apostle Paul answered that in the New Testament. Yes, I am my brother's keeper. I am responsible to not hurt them needlessly. I'm responsible to not hurt them for my own pleasure. Words can cut sharper than any knife. Please be careful in what you say, particularly if you carry the testimony of being a Christian. You are responsible to not hurt people.

I used to be involved in a lot of practical jokes and I had a real sharp tongue. I was a master of sarcasm at one time. I pray that God has taken that away from me. I don't want to be an offense to anyone.

## CHAPTER FORTY

## BE SURE YOUR SINS WILL FIND YOU OUT

Years ago I was involved in law enforcement aviation. I was the aircraft commander for Richland County Sheriff's Department. I flew Air 10, a patrol aircraft. We got involved with a lot of things. We assisted in high speed chases within our own department plus others, highway patrol and all. That set me up for a situation where I just stumbled on to something and it was quite interesting.

I guess I've always been considered a maverick, even before I went to Alaska. My pastor at the church I was attending at the time was having a missionary speaker who had been his seminary roommate and longtime friend. He was a missionary- at- large in a main line denomination. The pastor asked if the fellow could stay with us when he came. He felt like the guy would be more comfortable in our surroundings because I was pretty relaxed and sort of a non-conformist at the time, I guess you'd say.

Well, he came and he stayed with us. He ate dinner with us on the first evening. He said he wanted to take a walk in the woods, which we had about 600 acres of woods right behind our house at that particular time. It was Columbia Bible College property. He took a walk down through the woods, just relaxed and meditated and came back up and said he was ready to go preach.

He went off and got there about a half hour to 45 minutes before service time and talked with people and greeted people. He was a very sociable fellow. Then, just a few minutes before service time, he disappeared. Directly, he came back and entered the church through the back door straight onto the platform. He did his part in the service. Well, this happened several nights in a row. They were having five nights of missionary meetings Monday through Friday. It was either Wednesday or Thursday night I guess when I was about to leave for service and I got a call out to assist South Carolina Highway Patrol in a high-speed chase. They were chasing somebody and he circled around a bunch of places and they figured sooner or later he was going to dump the car and run and they wanted air support to try and locate him.

I headed for the airport. I got old 62 Romeo up. I was just about to pass over the church when Highway Patrol called the radio room and told them they had the guy in custody and they didn't need me anymore, I could just 1022 or I could just disregard, I could put the airplane away and go about my business. Well, it was just before service time and I was right over the church and I made some slow lazy circles, just looking at the church.

The missionary- at- large had a car that was very easy to spot. I believe it was red with a white top, if I recall correctly. In about my second circle I watched it take off. I decided I would follow it to see where he went. So I'm overhead 1,500 feet just taking slow, easy circles watching him. He goes down about two blocks and takes a right turn and pulls in and stops. Well, they were tree-lined streets and I couldn't see a whole bunch, but in just a fraction of a second after it stopped I saw a red glow in the vehicle. I just watched. A few minutes later there were a few showers of sparks beside the vehicle. The vehicle cranked up and he went back to the church and went in and had his service.

The next night after dinner the guy wanted to take his meditation walk down in the woods. I told him I wanted to walk with him, I enjoyed the woods. I enjoyed the outdoors. He was rather uncomfortable. We started walking and there, just out of sight of the house, was a tree stump with a bunch of cigarette butts around it. I told him to go ahead and sit down, light up man, relax. He looked at me with this terrified expression. He said, "How did you know?" I said, "Well, it's a long story." I told him what had happened and how I happened to know and promised him I would never name him and tell his secret.

I won't name him still. I don't even know if he's alive and well. I haven't heard anything about him in 20 years. He was a good bit older than me at the time, so if he's alive today he's probably pushing 90.

It was so funny. He called the pastor by name and he said he didn't know. He said he knows I like my privacy and I wander off and get out of the way, but he doesn't know what's going on. He said they were roommates in college. He never caught him and never found out.

He shared with me another story related to his smoking. He was a seminary student and he and his roommate got assigned to preach. One would preach in the morning and one in the evening at a little church that was without a pastor, and then they'd drive back to the seminary on Monday and start classes on Tuesday. He said he smoked for many, many years and he had a terrible time when he had a nicotine fit. One day they were going down a back woods road in Louisiana. He was the passenger and his roommate was driving. He'd run out of cigarettes and he desperately needed to get some cigarettes. He just couldn't figure how he was going to do this because there wasn't any way to get shed of his roommate, at least until they got to where they were going to be preaching.

He saw a sign for a bar and he said the wheels started turning. He said that it was the only business out there in the boondocks and he figured they'd sell cigarettes. And he'd figured out the perfect way to get there. He asked his roommate, " I hate to ask you to do this, but I need to use the restroom so bad it hurts and the only place coming up is this bar that we've seen several signs for. Would you mind stopping at the bar and let me use the restroom?" He said that as quick as the car came to a stop he jumped out and ran in and used the restroom. But as we all know, if you've been on a long trip and one person runs in to use the restroom, as soon as they get out that other person has got to get in there. So he was counting on his roommate running in there and using the restroom. Just as quick as he did, the seminary student ran over to the bar and said he needed two packs of Lucky Strike hard pack. He had to have the hard pack so that he could hide them without getting them crushed.

The bartender looked at him and said, "Mr. I don't have Lucky Strikes. I don't have the hard pack." The seminary student just sighed. He said,

"I've done everything to quit." Here was the student preacher telling the bartender that he was trying to quit. The bartender looked him right in the eye and said, "Have you ever tried praying about it"? The seminary student didn't bother to tell the bartender what his calling in life was or what he was doing. He just went on and lived without a cigarette that weekend.

I don't know if he ever did quit. I hope he did. A lot of times we do things and we're so sure nobody will ever find us out. We had a president in these United States that got involved in a whole bunch of private things that came out. There are other people in politics and full-time ministry who have had similar incidents. But you know, when Jesus promised "Lo I am with you always" it should also remind us that He's not just there for company, He's there watching everything we do. He's aware of whatever we do. You haven't fooled God. If you've come to the point in your life where you have asked Jesus Christ into your life and asked God to forgive you your sins, they're all forgiven whether anyone in the world catches up with them or not. They were forgiven when the first drop of blood fell from that cross on Calvary's mountain. We do sometimes have to do accountings. We may have to make things right with other people. We may have to just tell God that we're sorry and we want to turn from that sin. Some people take I John 1:9, "If we confess our sins, He is faithful and just to forgive us our sins and to cleanse us from all unrighteousness." to mean that they need to confess every sin every time they do it. If you read that carefully, that's a one-time event. You come when the Holy Spirit convicts you of your sin and you ask Him to forgive. And just like Peter, when Jesus told him he needed his feet washed because he was defiled by the world, we need to come to that point of turning away from the sin, telling God we're sorry for the sin. We don't have to list everything and be fearful that if we don't include some sin it won't be forgiven. They are all forgiven, but we need to keep God's attitude about sin.

A Christian can commit every sin that the lowest sinner without Christ can. The only difference is the Christian can't enjoy it because the spirit of God will convict him, will make him uncomfortable, will admonish him and encourage him to come back. God does discipline us to turn us away from our sins. His discipline is corrective. It's like the parent that spanks a child. One radio preacher says that God will take you to the wood shed, but once he's adopted you into his family he'll never cast you out.

Praise God. I'm so glad I'm a part of the family of God and my sins were forgiven at Calvary's Cross and I accepted that back in that little church in Streator, Illinois when I was just a kid.

I have had a lot of things I had to go talk to God about since. I've asked him to change my heart so that I didn't enjoy the wrong that I did. God has blessed me. I trust that you're walking with Him. Put Jesus Christ in your life and he'll show you what you need to put away to be a clean vessel for His service. By His grace we're saved. By His grace we live. By His grace he uses us even when we fail, even when we sin, but we don't want to live in that sin knowingly. God bless you as you walk with God.

## CHAPTER FORT-ONE

## WOUNDED SOLDIER

Paul tells us that we're in spiritual warfare as Christians and this is true in our everyday life. Sometimes the wounded soldiers who are in full-time Christian ministry are more obvious than others. I went through my Bible training. I went through my flight training and mechanics training. I went to Alaska. I went with the intention of being a missionary pilot but a number of things changed during our first few days there. God made it plain that he wanted me involved in a church planting ministry helping some struggling churches in the Copper River basin. While he did use my flight experience and flight training and maintenance of aircraft to reach out and build bridges to some men in the community and get them involved, bringing them into the chapel and to Jesus Christ as their Lord and Savior, my primary function was as a village missionary. Most of the stories in this book come from that time.

As is so often true in warfare, there are casualties. I went to war, spiritual warfare. I went with full intention of making a lifetime career change and dedicating the rest of my working life to service of the Lord in Alaska or wherever He called at any particular time. It didn't work out that way because of a number of things. There were difficulties in the family that caused me to really consider and to deal with the passage of scripture where Paul asks Timothy if a man cannot rule his own family well, how can he rule the house of God.

It became obvious my family wasn't in the order it needed to be in and I was dealing with the problems. As time went on, I found it necessary to read that passage to each chapel, the Chistochina Chapel and also the Slana Chapel, and that was the introduction to my resignation as their pastor.

The mission had asked us to go for extensive family counseling and I left with the intention of going through that, possibly for as much as a year, and fully intending to go back into full-time Christian service. I was hoping in Alaska because that was where my heart was, but wherever God called, wherever He opened the door. Because of difficulties within the family that needed to be resolved before I could go into a pastoral situation again we were leaving the field.

As we left, my wife and son needed to go to Portland. He had had an operation at the Shriner's Crippled Children's Hospital. He had to go there for his checkup before he was released after leg surgery. The school bus that we were using to haul everything out was not really economical. In fact, over the 4,200 miles it averaged about seven-and-a-half miles to the gallon and funds were limited. So they took the car and they headed for Portland and a day later Lou Riddley and I headed down the Alcan on a 1973 International school bus. The previous chapter entitled "Leaving Out" tells you about that adventure. It became obvious that family counseling was not going to work because all of the family wasn't going to be available for it. A number of things transpired and it became obvious that we were not going to survive as a family.

So I went back to Alaska and filed for a divorce there. It was one of the hardest things I've ever done in my life. I don't like divorce. I don't like that way out, but there was no option at that particular time. And many counselors, who knew both my wife and me and had dealt with it, agonized over it, cried over it and prayed over it, advised me that that was what needed to be done.

So as that process started, I was in Alaska. Normally the divorce would take place in four to six weeks. It was my intention to hang around Alaska and see what I could find to do in the line of work and see if maybe I had missed God's purpose. Maybe He had something there for me to do that I could remain on as an employee of some business or organization and still carry on and deal with the Alaskan, and particularly the native people for whom God had given me a love.

As the Lord would have it, after the time of filing of the divorce, the civil judge in that area passed away. In Alaska they just freeze civil matters until there's a new judge appointed. It's not a real quick process. I did come back to South Carolina and went to work at the Anderson County Sheriff's Department at that time. The court determined the date of the final hearing and notified me by mail that we were going to have a conference call that would be a trial in a family court setting with the judge in Alaska and myself in South Carolina and my wife, also in South Carolina at that time. Though I wasn't sure exactly where she was, she had filed an answer with them and given them a phone number to reach her.

As the Lord would have it, the day of the hearing was one year to the day when I had had to resign as pastor of Chistochina Chapel and Slana Chapel. Being divorced and being involved in service in a Christian church is a difficult position. I was truly a wounded soldier and I was bitter. I had gone to serve God and I felt like God let me down. I was angry with God. I told my father, who is still my number one spiritual counselor and a man that I greatly admire for his love of the Lord and the way he serves and the wisdom that God has given him.

I told Dad that I was mad at God and he, in his usual fashion, advised me to be very careful about saying such a thing. I thought about Indiana Jones who went in search of the Ark when he said something along that same line. His father slapped him across the face and said that was blasphemy. It was not intended for blasphemy. I told my dad probably the only thing dumber than being mad at God was trying to lie to Him about it.

I attended several different churches and I was not comfortable in any of them, didn't feel welcomed. In the middle of trauma, moving 4,200 miles, taking a 40 percent pay cut, losing a wife and a lot of my sources of income, and a lot of other material things, losing contact with my son, everything just didn't feel normal. My pastor, Butch Morrison, cautions about feelings, but in the middle of the trauma feeling does play a big part.

Finally I came upon the New Covenant Baptist church that was meeting on McDuffie Street and I started attending there. I talked with a number of folks who very much loved the Lord, had gone through all kinds of trauma and had found that God was faithful, and they encouraged me to trust Him and keep looking to him; that He was not done with me yet just because of this situation or because of the divorce.

I started in counseling and they use a little chart and they value different things in your life with a point value. Somewhere around eight or nine points they say you become a definite suicide risk. They added up the trauma that was going on in my life and found I had 27 points. I was messed up. I dealt with all kinds of things that you wouldn't normally think a Christian missionary would go through.

Because of lack of a vehicle, I ended up hitchhiking, depending on friends to borrow vehicles to get places. Keep in mind I'm now in a town where I don't have many friends because I'd never lived in Anderson before. I just know a few people who had been in Columbia that were now in Anderson.

I had picked up a $500 Pontiac station wagon. I would advise you if you only have $500 to spend on a car, just go ahead and hitchhike because after spending that $500 and you bought a $500 car, you're going to be hitchhiking anyway, but that's another story.

I was dealing with a number of mechanical problems with that. As I struggled to get it fixed, a number of the tools I needed were not available to me. My son had taken a small hand toolbox that basically had the tools I needed to fix the Pontiac. After skinning my knuckles and sliding out from under the car, very much angry, sitting up quickly, bumping my forehead on the frame because I wasn't out all the way yet, I went in the house.

I got the bleeding stopped on my hand and my forehead and was not thinking too logically. I loaded up the .44 Magnum and put it in a shoulder holster and realized that hitchhiking with that outfit probably wasn't going to be real successful. It was still warm weather but the only jacket I had at the time was a black jacket. So I put on a black jacket and I don't know what I thought was going to happen, but the chances are that at 110 in the shade and no shade, people are not going to stop and pick up a guy wearing a black jacket.

I set out to cure some of my problems. As I opened the door of 106 Powell Road to start my trip my pastor, Butch Morrison, was standing there on the porch. He had just come up and hadn't had time to knock on the door. He looked me right in the eye and said, "Is God pleased at what you're fixing to do?" Well, I did the only logical thing I could do. I shut the door and locked it. I stomped around the house for a little while and thought about this whole thing. I took the jacket off. I sat on the bed and thought a bit. I took the pistol out and unloaded the pistol. I took the holster off and put it away and went back to the door and sure enough Butch Morrison was still standing there. He had no idea what I was fixing to do. He didn't know what I had on under the jacket. He just knew that God had sent him there and he just said what God told him to say.

We talked for quite a while. Butch is a very gifted counselor and he wanted to counsel me dealing with forgiveness and bitterness and I told him that wasn't a problem, I had enough of that to last a lifetime; not the counseling, the bitterness. Butch knew the situation with my wife and a number of people who were in various leadership positions within the mission and active missionaries who concealed the truth from me about a lot of things that they knew. They had their reasons, and by God's grace I have left it at that, but at that particular time I was still struggling with it.

Butch talked about the chair and he recommended when you're dealing with somebody that you can't talk to face-to-face and you're dealing with something you hold against them, he recommended setting a chair there, visualizing that person in the chair, telling them what you held against them, what the problem was, what your feelings were and then committing that to God and telling them and God that as an act of your will you would forgive them through God's grace and God's strength and leave it be.

Well, I wasn't able to start with my wife. I started with several other missionaries and a number of other folks and friends that had been involved in deceiving me one way or the other, either inadvertently or by design because they didn't want to tell me what was really happening at the time. Apparently a number of other people knew how extensive the family problems were. But I started and I went through all of those. And then in the early morning hours one Saturday morning I got to the point where I mentally put my ex-wife in the chair and I told her all of the things that had me really riled up that had brought us to that point. I told her as an act of my will, by God's grace, in His strength I was committed to Him and I would forgive her.

When I finished that God said, "Al, can I sit in the chair?" And I struggled with that for a long time. Finally, I told God what I was mad about, how I was hurt. I felt I had gone to war and come home a wounded soldier. So many struggles that took place I felt like never should have come into a Christian family. I told Him I forgive Him. God said, "Al, sit in the chair."

I had to get up and walk around and prance around and go on. I couldn't do that for the longest time. Finally at about 2 or 2:30 on Saturday morning I sat in the chair and I verbalized where I was angry with myself and my failures and I asked God to overcome them. Because of God's grace He had already forgiven them; I had to forgive myself. When I did that I went to bed and slept peacefully. I don't know that I've lost a whole night's sleep since then.

The chair is not the magic; God's grace is the magic. It's what brings us forgiveness; it's what allows us to forgive others; it's what carries us through all the struggles of life; it's what allows us to still serve our Lord and Savior Jesus Christ.

I love the song "He didn't throw the clay away". God put me on a shelf for a period of time. God's still actively involved in my life and allows me to serve Him because of His grace and I bless Him for it.

I hope you have a chair. If you've got someone you can't deal with face-to-face and there's something burning in your soul go to God with it. If necessary, visualize that person, talk to them, tell them, and then as an act of your will before God forgive them and go on. God's got something for you to do as long as you're alive.

## CHAPTER FORTY-TWO

# GREAT IS THY FAITHFULNESS

That's a beautiful song, "Great is Thy Faithfulness Oh God Our Father". I love that song. It was the school hymn of Philadelphia College of Bible and it was awesome to listen to 500 Bible College students sing it in harmony. It touches my heart yet.

I've heard it sung on the mountain tops in Alaska and I've heard it sung in camps. I've heard it sung at the Bible College. Of course, every good Baptist church will sing it sometime or another. It expresses a truth that should never get old no matter how often we hear the song.

Jesus Christ became my Savior when I was about seven years old in a little Primitive Methodist Church in Streator, Illinois. Reverend Russell Kingsley led me to the Lord. He was a conference evangelist for the Primitive Methodist conference, which my father later served as a pastor until his retirement. It was the denomination I grew up in.

I recall the night Reverend Kingsley was preaching. We'd gone to several of the meetings and my father had either just recently gotten saved or was about the get saved. We were saved right about the same time and I didn't write down the date when I was saved. I didn't realize how important it would be in my life.

He was a great singer. He sang that night, "I've anchored my soul in the haven of rest", in the little church with no air conditioning. Of course we're talking about 1951, the windows were open. It was warm. In the Midwest you'd get pop-up storms every once in a while, and we had one of the most violent storms with lightening, thunder and rain. They had to close the windows to keep the rain out and partially to keep out the noise of the thunder.

That impressed me. Here he is singing about anchored in the haven of rest and the wild waves, so to speak, were really blowing outside.

I don't know what he preached about that night, but I do know that when he offered the invitation I knew that I needed a Savior and I wanted Jesus Christ in my life, not just as my Savior but as my Lord. I went forward and kneeled at that altar rail right next to the organ on the right side of the church. The church has been remodeled and all that's changed, but I kneeled right there on the right.

Reverend Kingsley himself came and spoke with me. There were a number of counselors. Several people came, I don't remember how many.

Reverend Kingsley talked with me. He's now gone to be with the Lord, but he made an impression on me and God used him as my spiritual birth father. As time went on, my father grew in the Lord and studied, memorizing a great deal of scripture. He taught me the importance of scripture and of memorizing it, hiding God's word in my heart that I might not sin against Him.

I was blessed in the early years. Dad went into the ministry on my ninth birthday, May 17th, 1954. We left Streator in a 1954 Ford that Dad had bought brand new. It was about $900, if I remember correctly hearing the story. They had sold the house that they had recently built. They put everything in a little, probably five-by-eight two-wheel mounted utility trailer. They pulled it behind that Ford and moved to Lawrence, Massachusetts.

Daddy was a pastor for two churches there, the Salem Street Primitive Methodist Church, which is the one we lived by right in Lawrence, and then the Tyler Street Primitive Methodist Church, which was in Methuen, probably seven to nine miles away.

A lot of things happened in my life right there. Daddy preached at Tyler Street in the morning, came back and taught Sunday school at Salem Street and then preached at Salem Street. Then they had a combined evening service. One Sunday a month it was at Tyler Street and the other Sundays it was at Salem Street because it was the larger church and the larger number of people.

They had a great relationship between the churches, and I think Daddy helped foster that because he believes in the fellowship of all believers and working together for the cause of Christ.

I used to sleep on the piazza, as they called it, which was an upstairs porch. It didn't have a roof over it; it had a little overhang from the roof itself, but it was an open-air porch. I called it camping out and I loved to do that.

I'd lay there and watch the planes take off from North Andover Airport, as they came right up over the trees. I can remember the DC-3's, Douglass DC-3, the king of the tail draggers, big twin engine, coming up over the trees and watching the landing gear retract as they took off. I wanted to learn to fly!

Also, as we would go to Tyler Street we'd go parallel to Merrimack River for a little ways. We passed a sea plane base where people were taking instruction and learning how to fly sea planes. That, again, kept me interested in aviation.

It was in 1955 that five missionaries were killed by the Auca Indians, Jim Elliott being one of them. Jim Elliott's life story <u>Through Gates of Splendor</u> was made into a movie. Of course, Jim Elliott was the missionary pilot who helped spearhead the effort to reach these stone-age Indians and bring them to the Lord.

I told my mother after watching that that I wanted to be a missionary pilot in Alaska. Many things happened and I never got the chance to get a flying lesson in my earlier days.

I moved around the countryside. I had a relapse of rheumatic fever and God worked in His own special way through an old country doctor, old Dr. Worley. He treated me with penicillin three times a day and monitored my temperature and had them keep a chart. If my temperature went up, Mom was supposed to call him and he would do whatever it took to get my temperature down.

We moved out of Wilkes-Barre, Pennsylvania and went to Providence, Rhode Island. Daddy went up there with the Primitive Methodist Home Mission Board to try to help a struggling little church get back on its feet and independent enough to support a pastor.

When we got up there, I remember walking with Daddy as he went around and did a survey. He was one of the first I knew to use a survey as a contact point. He would knock on doors and when people answered the door he'd ask them, " Could I ask you a few questions? I just want some information on the community." And then he would ask them about their church contacts, and if they didn't have any, he'd immediately invite them to the Primitive Methodist Church.

He finished up by asking them about their relationship with Jesus Christ and talked with people about the Lord there. That was my earliest view of a pastor at work. He would pastor his own, but he also worked as an evangelist reaching out to others. God impressed that on me.

Anyway, it just so happened that during that one year we were in Providence, Rhode Island we got the Sunday paper, and of course it always had these little special things and inserts. There was an article on Dr. Fineburg. I don't know his first name, but he was the world's leading authority on rheumatic fever. He was within about three miles of where we lived. He was a very, very expensive specialist at that time and we weren't making much money. I don't know what the salary was in Providence, but it wasn't much.

My mother was a Scot. Her mother had been born in Glasgow and came over from Scotland and she had learned to be frugal and she learned how to save. Something in this newspaper article said that an initial visit with Dr. Fineburg was $100. Momma had read this and saved.

I'll never forget, she sat down one Sunday dinner when the whole family was together after church, she said: "We're going to take Alan to see

Dr. Fineburg. I want him checked out. This is supposed to be the best man. This may be what God brought us to Providence, Rhode Island for. I want to know that he's been looked at by the best, who is right here available to us." Daddy said, "Well, that would be great, but don't you remember it is $100 for an initial visit?" And Momma reached up in the cupboard and pulled out a $100 bill.

It was the first one I ever saw. But she had saved and she'd gotten her savings together and changed it to a $100 dollar bill. Momma taught me that the larger the bills you keep, the easier it is to save money. If you walk out with ten ones, you'll spend nine of them. If you walk out with a $100 bill you stop and think before you break that, so she constantly tried to work up to the largest bills she could have just for saving purposes.

Well, to make a long story short, she had already made the appointment and we went to see Dr. Fineburg. He was a very gracious man. I don't know anything about his relationship with his Messiah. He was a Jewish doctor. We filled out the information and Dad put that he was a pastor and put the address and everything.

We went in and we had the consultation and he did some tests. He said, "This boy is healthy." He said, "I'd love to talk to the doctor who was treating him because he has virtually no side effects other than a very slight heart murmur." We were just so blessed, but then as we went out and Daddy went up to the counter to give him that $100 bill, the doctor waved at him and said, "Thank you, Reverend, no charge." He sent us on.

We ate steak that night. Momma spent the $100 bill. It was such a blessing. I was never in real good health growing up. I'd had polio, and I guess I need to tell that story too. I was taken to the Streator Hospital when I was four-and-a-half years old. My left leg was three-quarters of an inch shorter than my right leg, and they had confirmed that it was polio. The doctors didn't know what to do for that. They put me in a whirlpool and tried to ease the pain. The leg was very painful and stiff.

My parents went to the Reverend Keeley's house, the pastor at the Primitive Methodist Church at that time, and they determined they were going to pray all night for my healing. They went to praying and at about 2 o'clock in the morning old Mr. Hall, and I can't tell you his first name, but he was a dear saint of God who could pray for days, but he jumped up and started singing the doxology, "Praise God from whom all blessings flow".

He told them it was time for everyone to go home, you-all have to go to work tomorrow, you-all need to get some rest. They said, no, we're praying all night. He said, "When God answers prayer, it's time to thank Him and go on." He insisted that God had answered prayer and that I was going to be healed.

Well, they didn't want to leave, they wanted to pray. Old Mr. Hall, being a man of his convictions, as I understand it, of course I was in the hospital, but he took a broom and ran them out of the parsonage. Dad went to the doctor and asked him to give me another test and he said, no, he's got polio and there's not much that's going to change that and we don't know much about it, and just put him off.

Well, he was persistent. The doctor finally consented and they did another spinal tap and took spinal fluid and checked it.

The doctor came back and said, "I don't know what happened. I know this boy had polio, but he doesn't have polio now." Three days after I was admitted, I walked out of St. Mary's Hospital in Streator, Illinois.

Still, every once in a while when I get tired, I limp on my left leg, but I believe God left that as a reminder of His faithfulness so that I wouldn't forget.

I swore Daddy had gypsy blood in him, but he was a Primitive Methodist preacher and they moved you right often. Daddy was constantly taking churches that were not doing so well just to try and help them because he loved the outreach part of ministry. Then he would move on.

I can recall they closed the Providence church after that first year. They said it just wasn't worth keeping it open, and I remember helping Daddy nail the door shut. I think that that took a toll on him because he believed that God was faithful and he didn't understand why that church was allowed to die.

I don't know either. I don't know what happened to that building or anything about that, but even in the death of a church God has a purpose.

So we left Providence and went to Girardville, Pennsylvania, down in the coal country. I had some good times there. I learned to drive there. I went to Girardville High School my sophomore year of high school. I went to Ashland High School my junior year of high school. And then as the Lord would have it my senior year, Ashland, Girardville and Butler High School, the three rivals, were joined together into a joint high school and I graduated from Ashland Area Joint High School.

I just returned from the 40-year class reunion. I got a photograph of the 37 of us that attended. I sent a message to Sam and Jenny who had sent me the picture. We don't look bad after 40 years of wear and tear.

God used those experiences in the high school days. I was involved in the Youth for Christ Bible Club there. People who had been rivals forever molded together into a new school and a new heart and were able to make life-long friendships.

I went through some problems in my teenage years. I got a driver's license and I thought a car was a great means of transportation, but the faster you could go the more fun it was. In those days I'd race anything. I raced that '54 Ford that Daddy still had.

I was in a wreck with one of the high school football stars and the cheerleaders started calling me the roadrunner, beep, beep roadrunner when I'd walk by them because I had run into Freddie Spelus, one of the favorite high school football players. I walked away from that without any severe damage. I tore up a good car and Daddy traded it not long after that. I found that God kept me safe in all kinds of circumstances, even when I didn't use my own good sense.

I graduated from high school and had been working for several years doing work in a photographic dark room, Panmont Photo Service.

It's now closed up and Mr. Kellshaw, the owner has passed away. He became a special friend. He was my first boss who paid me regular paychecks and sent me out on different jobs.

I had saved my money, and I applied to Philadelphia College of Bible, intending to study for a ministry.

I went to study, but I still liked to play. I didn't have a car to play with in Philadelphia, but there is a whole book of stories of practical jokes and experiences at Philadelphia College of Bible. I spent a lot more time playing than I did studying.

I started my freshman year working as night watchman. That was my first involvement in anything in law enforcement, which ended up as a career I have been in for 29 years. I'm 58 years old. I've been a cop half of my life.

I was put on probation, academic probation. I lost my 4D or ministerial student deferment. Keep in mind we're talking about 1966, Viet Nam is hot. President Johnson helped educate the world. He sent college educated people all over the world. Most of them ended up in Viet Nam or in that area of the world. I was drafted and went to Fort Rucker, Alabama ultimately. I spent one year, 11 months and 28 days. I say I was a career soldier, but it was a very brief career. I was involuntary service, US52985832. I still remember that service number because they wouldn't let me eat until I could recite it. It's well impressed in my mind.

I got married right there at Fort Rucker. I married a lady who was in service. I used to say that she outranked me and ordered me to marry her. She got out of the service when she was expecting our first son, David Alan, who even as I write this chapter of the book I'm on my way to see. I haven't seen him or spent any time with him for six years because of a lot of things. He just moved from Denver, Colorado out to St. Mary's, Georgia, right down there near Jacksonville, Florida.

I went back to Illinois when I was getting out the service. I couldn't get medical insurance and had a pregnant wife. I didn't have enough money to do anything. When we left there the boy was 18 months old. The Lord opened the door for me to go to Columbia Bible College, Columbia, South Carolina.

We headed south again. Being a brilliant student, I crammed my four years of college into ten years, starting in 1963, graduating in 1973. I went through some experiences there that are probably another book by themselves. I don't know if they'll ever get written, but that's not what it's about.

I graduated there and a few days later I ran into Sonny Clark, who was a lieutenant at Richland County Sheriff's Department. He had just gotten saved and he asked me if I had a church yet. I said, "No, you know I only graduated three days ago and don't know exactly how that's going to happen or how soon." By this time I was in the Southern Baptist Convention and I was a licensed local preacher with them. I had done some interim preaching and filling in.

Sonny said, "We need Christian cops. Go down and see Captain Johnny Fulmer and put in an application at Richland County Sheriff's Department. So to appease Sonny and get him off my back, I went down and took the test, filled out an application. It's real funny, you know, a lot of boys grow up and want to be a cop. I never thought about being a cop. I wanted to be a preacher. I wanted to be a pilot. I wanted to be a cowboy. It was too late to be an Indian, but I would have wanted to be one of them if I could.

It ended up that I only missed one question on the test. Captain Fulmer, who later became a very dear friend, asked me when I could start. I started waffling and he said, "Well, do you want a job or don't you?" I said, "Well, yeah, I got a wife and a kid and she's in college and I need a job. He said, "Okay, when can you start?

I started the next Monday. The Lord was good. I spent 15 years there. I spent a lot of time preparing for what God would do in Alaska where the thoughts and most of the ideas of this book come from.

It was there that Sheriff Frank Powell appointed me chaplain and taught me a lot about working with people in trauma. He taught me how to deal with situations, not just as a cop, but as a preacher and a cop. I had the privilege of leading a number of people to the Lord during my time there because of circumstances that God opened up.

I also got promoted and had a straight day job and got better pay coming in and was able to take flying lessons. I started my flying lessons when I was 34 years old. I remember when Ken Moyer got out that old 1973 Cessna 150. The "N" number was 18017. He told me to take it around the pattern by myself. I took off and it was a spiritual experience for me. I had wanted to be a missionary pilot. Even in this first solo take-off I said, "God, this is great. Please let me do it on a foreign field for you." I was able to end up flying in Alaska, which of course is the United States, but it was a long way from South Carolina. God opened that door.

We left there, froze my retirement at 15 years and fully intended to go full time as a missionary for the rest of my life. As you saw from the previous chapters, I went through some problems and faced a divorce, which took me out of the ministry and off of the mission field.

As I came to Anderson, a place where I knew only two or three people, I called Mike Temple, who had been my captain at Richland County and asked him if he had an opening. He got me an interview with the sheriff. I flew down to Anderson and talked briefly with the sheriff. God opened that door and I went to work there with the intent of finishing ten more years in law enforcement and being able to draw my retirement at 25 years, going back into full-time Christian work of some kind and hopefully going back to Alaska.

I had already calculated what the retirement would pay me and was pretty sure that I'd be able to live in Alaska on that retirement. I was putting it all together mentally.

I flew back to Alaska to load the bus that we purchased to transport our belongings because you couldn't get a U-Haul truck coming out of Alaska at that particular time. On the road down I saw the family disintegrate and didn't have a permanent address for a while. When I finally sent Glennallen Post Office a change of address, I was blessed. You don't know what it is to not get mail for a month and then all of a sudden it all comes together. Guess what comes, bills, big bills, overdue bills.

One from Visa caught my attention right away and it said your account is $1,297 overdrawn, please remit immediately.  That was in the first batch of mail that I got.  I wanted to change my address again and send it somewhere else.

I looked at that and just threw it on the kitchen table there at 106 Powell Road and said there's no hope.  I had taken a 40 percent pay cut.  I didn't even have a paycheck coming for two weeks yet.  I had to move into a house.  I wasn't able to pay the deposit, but Ms. Helen Daracott, who has now gone to be with the Lord, was a very precious lady to me and she encouraged me and allowed me to move in without paying the deposit at the time because of my situation.

Here I was, oh well.  I went to work the next day, came home, reached in the same mailbox that I got the bills out of.  I pulled out $1,200 in checks that people had sent.

I cashed the checks, went ahead and paid the overage so that it was down to the limit, cancelled the card, wrote them an explanation of why I was doing it and why I wasn't going to be doing anymore charging and hopefully nobody else was going to be doing anymore charging to avoid the bankruptcy syndrome.  Again, they were gracious to me and in God's goodness they gave me a new Visa card after I had paid off that account.

I had a day when I got up and found I was driving a four-speed, four cylinder '85 Chevrolet Cavalier with a bad valve.  There was no way I could do a valve job myself with the tools I had.  I was working and I couldn't get where I needed to go.  I finally took it over to Firestone.  They were the nearest place so that I could walk home. I told them to go ahead and fix it and I would pay for it when I was able. Of course, I didn't have a credit card anymore.

I came home from work the next day, the day that it was supposed to be done, and there in the mailbox was a check from George Schultz, a missionary friend from Alaska. Two of his children had gotten their dividend checks from the state of Alaska and God had impressed on them that I needed some help and they sent me $100. I cashed that check and paid the $85 that I owed on the car. It was just God's faithfulness moving the hearts of children to provide.

I never missed a meal. People who know me know that I need to miss a few; I need to lose a little weight, but God has been good. Any dieting I've done has been for dietary reasons, not economic. Though I have seen when there was no money in the house, God worked in various ways to bring in what I needed. Somebody would come by and ask me, hey, do you want to go out to eat and I'd say no and they'd say, come on I'll buy. Off I would go, and sometimes I'd eat a steak dinner when I wouldn't have had peanut butter and jelly in the house, because of God's faithfulness.

I moved on in some other areas too. Keep in mind I relocated 4,200 miles and I left the two churches that are dearest to me. I left as their pastor but I finally got connected with New Covenant Baptist Church, which was the root of Midway Community Church, where I am now serving the Lord as a lay worker.

The spirit there on McDuffie Street was much the same as the Slana Chapel. They were a little more expressive, a little Pentecostal. Mike Noland was the prayer and praise leader. I love that man. I told the story of the church choosing to honor him for his volunteer service as our music director and prayer and praise team leader. He took no money for it; he just served the Lord and gave of his own time, energies and money to provide for the position.

Mike reminded me so much of taking off in Palmer, Alaska and circling up through the clouds and breaking out in the bright sunshine at the top. Mike's face just radiates the love of the Lord. Mike took me to his heart. Early on when I was mad at God, Mike had hugged me and thanked me for coming. He'd do everything he could to make me feel welcome, to talk to me, to help me in any way that he could. God used him, not only in my own life, but in that of Al Carver, who is also a dear friend who has gone to be with the Lord.

Al Carver had not been a regular in church for quite some time, but when he started coming Mike developed a good rapport with him. He had touched that man, and it was through Mike Noland and Butch Morrison and my own father, who had come to visit and had become a good friend of Al's, that Al ended up getting saved. Al would call Dad and talk to him now and again. He had some eye problems and never would get glasses and Dad sent him a large print Bible.

Even at that time, when I was mad at God, I was seeing God working in my own life and reaching out through others to me and through me to others and I realized that God was not finished with me yet.

*Great is Thy Faithfulness* is not just a song; it's a way of life. We need to understand that He is forever faithful. He promises that He will supply all our needs according to His riches in glory. Let me tell you, my bank account isn't much, but God's is unlimited and God has chosen to bless me spiritually, physically, emotionally, and financially. I'm probably better off now than I ever have been in my life.

I'm looking toward retirement and for the day when I'll be able to spend three days a week working on airplanes, which is probably the most favorite job I've had for secular work, and spending three days a week working in the church for the Lord.

I don't care what I do in the church. I don't have to be a counselor. I can be a janitor; I can be a yard man; I can do whatever. God has blessed me through His church and I want to serve Him through the church; whether it's a church here or a church on a foreign field.

I don't know what God has for me, but I know that if God calls you to it, He'll bring you through it. Because of my own life, I know that He will supply everything I need to go where He wants me to go and do what He wants me to do and to reach others for Himself.

Jesus Christ loves you. He died for you. He died for you so He could be your Savior. Come to Him. If you've never met Jesus Christ, ask Him to forgive you for your sins and ask Him to come into your life. Allow Him into your life to work through you for His honor and glory and for your well-being.

I don't believe in the "prosperity gospel." When you get saved, the devil is going to bug you like he never did before. Of course, you were in his family before you got saved, so why would he bother his own?

God does work for your well-being. In my case He has blessed me with some measure of finances that I'm able to do things that I want to do. I don't know how long that will be. I don't know that finances will always be an easy thing, but I do know that God is faithful and I'd rather have God providing my needs than any unlimited bank account this world has to offer. Money can get you into the wrong things. God will keep you in the right things if you'll walk with Him.

Butch Morrison preaches "The Exchanged Life". It comes from a verse in Galatians. "I am crucified with Christ; nevertheless I live, yet not I, but Christ liveth in me." My prayer for you is that Jesus Christ does live in your life.

Come to Him for salvation, but if you've known Him as the Savior and you've never allowed Him to live His life through you, oh, surrender to that. Let Him just fill your life. Let Him be your life because He's got a plan that's much better than anything you could dream up on your own. I promise you.

God bless you. Love you all.

**CHAPEL MAILBOX IN SNOW**

**CHISTOCHINA CHAPEL**

*INTERIOR, CHISTOCHINA CHAPEL*

*NELCHINA GLACIER*

**STAINED GLASS WINDOW, CHISTOCHINA PUBLIC SCHOOL**

**CHISTOCHINA LODGE, HAS SINCE BEEN DESTROYED BY FIRE**

## EPILOGUE

## BACK TO ALASKA

Sunday June 10, 2012: I got up, ate breakfast and went to church just like always, except I didn't get home again until Saturday July 7. Wow, what a trip.

I turned my car over to Mike Noland, a fellow elder in Midway Community Church and he drove me to Atlanta International Airport. I checked in with TSA for the first time since my last trip to Alaska in 1991, boarded Alaska Airlines and flew to SEA/TAC. I had a 4-hour layover so I went to find dinner. I ate the usual fare there in the airport.

Back on Alaska Airlines and on to Anchorage. It was my first time in Alaska since 1991.

My old neighbor, and best friend in Alaska, Chuck Hermans picked me up in his Ford F250 and off we went to Wasilla where I met Blue Sky, my 2006 Harley Davidson Road King Peace Officers' Edition. Chuck had found this bike for me in Arizona and then trucked it to Alaska and did some work on it, getting ready for a two week tour of Alaska and the trip back to South Carolina.

Chuck would be my guide, just like old times when he had cared for me as his pastor and friend when I was just Cheechaco. He would shepherd me down the Alaska Highway(we call it the Al-Can) to Dawson Creek, British Columbia then head back north and I would go on solo. That was the plan, but it changed. My Dad used to say "Life is what happens between your plans".

I sat on the bike and could ride it, but it was too high and I did not have my riding gear. I had shipped my cold weather gear, rain suit and boots to Chuck but they had not arrived. I rode in street clothes, loafers and a jacket borrowed from Chuck. I did have my gloves but probably did not need them. I have a 34 inch sleeve and Chuck is closer to 36 so my hands were covered.

The Harley had 4010 miles on it when I first sat on it. Chuck is a master mechanic and he had picked it up and installed new tires and a battery since it had not been ridden regularly for a number of years. Then he did a test ride and started tweaking it for the ride.

We slept for a few hours then headed for Denali Harley to get my mileage certified for Harley Owners Group awards. I would be eligible for the 1000 mile award before I left Alaska and the 5000 mile before I got to Anderson, SC. I waited and got them both at the same time when I got home and got Timms HD to file for me.

After that stop we headed for the Matanuska Family Restaurant. This is an important place because every morning retired people solve the problems of the world there. Chuck and Bev hang out there when they are in town. We had a great time and I met many of their friends.

We stayed just long enough to leave in a cold rain and 45 degrees at sea level. Unfortunately that would be the last time we were at sea level and as we climbed the mountains it got colder. We ended that trip in 32 degrees and freezing rain pounding on the helmet so hard I could not hear the engine. Oh what fun! Now I am questioning why I did not just make this a scenic trip and buy a Harley at home. Chuck was a great encouragement. Of course he rides in colder weather but I had not gotten acclimated yet. We stopped at Summit lodge and got a warm dinner and on Chuck's advice I drank a cup of warm water. It helped. We ran into some old friends form the Copper River Valley there and had a nice visit.

Back in the saddle and on to the Hub of Alaska at Glennallen. We gassed up, got a snack and headed for Chistochina.. The last 15 miles were the hardest with a rain now pouring. Chuck had to put my bike in the shop because of the unusual ramp arrangement and my short legs. Inside, Bev did her usual as the perfect hostess and great cook and made me glad to be back. I slept well that night and really felt at home.

Chuck isn't a man who sits still long. We got up the next morning and measured me, then the bike. Parts were ordered, then the wait. We did some local rides but I still did not have my riding gear and the bike was too high for me to ride comfortably.

I had a couple days to just wander around Chistochina. Things had changed. No generators in the back yard, a power station where the old lodge had been before it burned. A bed and breakfast is on the plot of land behind where the lodge had been. Chisto School is now closed, a pretty old building that is a ghost.

Chisto Chapel had not changed. The building itself held fond memories. I attended service on Sunday but it was different. The last time I was in that building I was the pastor and part of a family that had adopted me. Now all of the kids in Sunday School had been born since I left. Half of the adults did not know who I was. Old friends were there but busy at their duties. Visits were brief. I was the tourist with time on my hands and they were the ones who had things to do.

The population had grown. It was about 70 when I left, now there are probably 200 but the old small town feel is gone. Many of the new residents don't socialize like the old natives. Many of the Athabascan Elders are gone.

Posty's is the only store in town. Ernie and Barb Charlie are running it and have made it an asset to the area. They have gas, souvenirs, food and some clothing. They have a warm welcome that still sort of fits with Chisto.

Ernie's father, Jerry Charlie, is still around and active. We had several old style visits both at Posty's and Chuck and Bev's. He had been an encouragement when I first came to Chisto.

Chuck and I took several rides to visit and to stop by the Slana settlement and see the new Slana Chapel. The old one had burned just before I left in 1991.

Monday June 25 at 7:15: With a full load of baggage strapped to Blue Sky we set out for Dawson Creek Canada. Chuck was escorting me down the Al-Can and then he would head back north and I would head for Edmonton to visit Dave and Kathy Gotlob. I had wanted to do this but now it seemed like a bigger undertaking as I looked at miles of road and detours with pilot cars leading me through loose gravel.

Chuck is old Navy and his travel plans start at 7:15, kickstands up and rolling. He liked to ride out the first tank of fuel then somewhere after that he would stop for breakfast. I was Army and they say we travel on our stomach but Navy does that differently.

Shortly after we got into Canada we ran into a guy from Texas who was riding a Harley. He pulled a trailer but had lost a bolt for the hitch... Chuck's road handle is "Toolkit". Sure enough he had one that would work, and we started traveling together.

We got to Whitehorse, Yukon Territory and made camp. These guys were avid campers but I didn't do nearly as well at that.

Sure enough, up 6AM, shower, pull up the tent, pack the gear and be ready. At 7:15 kickstands up and hit the road. A bunch more detours that were worse than yesterday.

Ten hours later: Toad River. Winds were howling and I told the guys if I have to get up in the night I will never find my tent when I come back from the outhouse. They humored me. We got a cabin. Nice comfortable bed, watched a little TV but Yep, 6AM shower and pack. Seven- fifteen kickstand up, we are on the road again.

Chuck humored me one more time when we got to Fort Nelson. I really enjoyed the hotel there for breakfast which was great. We stopped early, but I liked it.

Suddenly: Mile Zero of the Alaska Highway. Dawson Creek, British Columbia. Chuck and I had a last dinner together and he headed north to his nephew's wedding. Gene had service to be done at

Harley Davidson so he went on to Grande Prairie and I holed up in Dawson Creek.

Guess what time I started. It wasn't 7:15! In fact I did not even see 7:15 on the clock, on purpose. I left there about 8:30 and met Gene in Grand Prairie. We had breakfast there and waited for the new tire to be installed. It took them a while. We hit the road at 1 PM and pushed to make Edmonton.

Dave and Kathy Gotlob had not changed. The food was great, the fellowship greater.

We had to hit the road early to miss bad weather in Calgary. We beat it, but not by much. We passed through Calgary on Gene's schedule and watched as the rain came in behind us.

I gassed up in Lethbridge with the last of my Canadian money and hauled for Sweet Grass, Montana.

It's not a good idea to cross the border at 5 PM on Friday. It was crowded and we had to wait. Dinner at Pizza Hut was great. Nothing is as American as Italian food.

Just for information, the total cost of the trans-Canada run; motels, food and fuel was $594 dollars Canadian. The exchange rate makes it wise to get the Canadian money at the bank and avoid having people at stores make up their own rates.

Great Falls Montana was the scene of my maintenance disaster on the trip out (see the Chapter on Leaving Out) but it was a good stop for Gene and me. We got a nice room, did laundry and watched US news and programing.

I guess Gene was more modern Navy as we did not leave until 8:15. I work better on that schedule.

We always watched for animals on the trip. I saw moose, caribou, bison, eagle, wolf and dall sheep. We saw one black bear but no grizzly. Believe it or not the only deer we saw was in downtown Billings at 2PM. Poor little doe got scared into the traffic and nearly got hit.

Gene and I stopped at the Battle of the Little Big Horn Memorial. I was surprised to see that most of the guides were Native Americans. They are still a proud people and certainly have a right to be. I am proud to have many friends in the Athabascan Community and even as a kid when we played cowboys and Indians I wanted to be the Indian.

We went on to Buffalo, Wyoming where Gene split off heading for Texas. He was a good traveling companion and he prayed for safety for each of us on our travels.

Well, here goes. I had never traveled on a motorcycle alone more than 900 miles from home and never on a road that I had not traveled in a car before. It was solo time. I had had company for half the trip. Now it is me, Blue Sky and the Lord. We had a good trip.

I stopped in Sturgis, the mecca of motorcycling, and toured the Museum. The Rally had not started yet so I pretty much had the town to myself.

I had an American steak at Jesse's Steakhouse and it was great. He owns a ranch and raises his own cattle, butchers his own meat and then sells it. It was outstanding.

I rode the Needles Highway in Custer State Park and truly enjoyed one of the most beautiful places on earth. I was not able to see Mt Rushmore because of the forest fires. They shut down that road when the visibility went down in the smoke.

It was at Lake Sylvan that I lost a set of keys. I had an Anderson County Sheriff Dept. Badge on them and I wanted the badge worse then I wanted the keys. In December I got a call from the department and Captain asked me if I had stopped in the park and if I had lost a set of keys. Five months later I got them back. God looks after the details and I thank Him for that.

I rode for a couple more days to get to Illinois and visit family. It was great, and after that stop it was roads I had traveled before and it was time to put it into the wind and head for home.

July 7th: I made it to the house. The return to Alaska was great. The Alaska trip on a motorcycle was complete on my bucket list.

I'm glad I got the time in Alaska. Glad to see old friends and places. Miss the old friends who are gone. I'm thankful that the close ones all knew Jesus as their Savoir and I will see them again.

"Shanan."

# ACKNOWLEDGEMENTS

This project was not a solo work. There were many people involved and I thank every one of you. I must first acknowledge Julie Ashworth who carefully and meticulously typed the transcript from my ramblings on a cassette tape recorder. I recorded these while I was traveling and you can imagine how difficult it was to unravel! Julie worked with me at the Anderson County Courthouse and very generously took on this assignment and did an excellent job. Thank you.

There were others who started on the project but one way or another were hindered from completing. I appreciate your efforts on my behalf as well. There were a lot of disappointments, but there was also encouragement as people learned of the project and offered their help.

I want to thank Betty Cameron, my editor. A friend for more than half of my life, her careful reading and putting things together in a more understandable fashion is greatly appreciated. I believe in degrees for literature and she is certainly a master at books. When you read this I believe you'll find it extremely readable, thanks to her, because my English ain't that great. David Cameron, Betty's husband, has been a spiritual mentor, advisor and counselor to me for many years. He took on the business end of this operation. I thank you so much.

There are many people who lived the stories with me I appreciate each one of them. Some of them are gone now but not forgotten. Some folks in Alaska kept in touch when I left and filled in the gaps. I appreciate them and I appreciate you the reader. It is my prayer that each one of you will enjoy this effort and appreciate God's grace in His mercy to all of us.

Yours in Jesus,
Alan L Pearce